# THE BATTLE
# FOR CORK

MILITARY HISTORY
OF THE IRISH CIVIL WAR

# THE BATTLE
# FOR CORK

## JULY–AUGUST 1922

JOHN BORGONOVO

SERIES EDITOR: GABRIEL DOHERTY

MERCIER PRESS
IRISH PUBLISHER – IRISH STORY

MERCIER PRESS

Cork

www.mercierpress.ie


© Text: John Borgonovo, 2011

© Foreword: Gabriel Doherty, 2011


ISBN: 978 1 85635 696 1


10 9 8 7 6 5 4 3 2 1


A CIP record for this title is available from the British Library

Printed and bound in the EU.

# CONTENTS

# Acknowledgements

This book was written with the assistance of a number of people. Thanks to Pat Gunn, who passed on a copy of his fascinating interview with his father George, an IRA veteran. Gerry White and Colman O'Mahony provided personal insights into their published work on these events, for which I am grateful. I would also like to thank Dr Donal Ó Drisceoil of the University College Cork (UCC) School of History for assistance with illustrations; Michael Murphy of the UCC Geography Department for generous map production; Cork Fire Brigade historian Pat Poland; Cork historian Antoin O'Callaghan; series editor Gabriel Doherty of the UCC School of History; and the staff at Mercier Press.

Kieran Burke and the staff at the Local Studies Department, Cork City Library, provided critical help. I would also like to acknowledge Commandant Victor Lange at the Military Archives, Dublin; the staff at the University College Dublin Archives; and Brian McGee and the team at the Cork City and County Archives. Thanks are also due to the Port of Cork for offering prompt access to its strongroom.

The National Archives of Ireland graciously granted permission to use the Hogan/Wilson photographs, which serve as an excellent documentary source for these events. Thanks to Sarah Buckley for offering her father's photographs for publication. I am also grateful to Tony McCarthy, who provided a photograph of 'Scottie' McKenzie Kennedy, and a copy of the Timothy Kennefick Coroner's Inquest, planting seeds that blossomed in this work.

Many thanks to Ronan Kirby and Denis Kirby, who offered

welcome local knowledge of Douglas/Rochestown, as well as a fruitful driving tour. I am also grateful to John Dennehy of Cobh for his expert knowledge of the port, and to Martin Buckley, formerly of the Irish Navy, for further harbour advice.

Historian Tom Mahon of Hawaii earns special kudos for graciously copying Captain Somerville's reports to the British Admiralty, which can be found in Kew National Archives. I am looking forward to Tom's upcoming book on the *Upnor* raid.

# LANGUAGE AND SOURCES

This book sets out to examine events in the city of Cork during July and August 1922, in the conventional phase of the Irish Civil War. Its structure and style are intended to appeal to a wide readership; it is not meant to offer the last word on Cork in the Civil War, or on the National Army's amphibious offensive during August 1922. *The Battle for Cork* seeks to answer the question: How did a city so closely identified with militant Irish Republicanism from 1917 to 1921 pass so easily into the hands of the Irish Free State? Events are viewed deliberately from a Cork perspective.

My use of language deserves a brief mention. I call members of the anti-Treaty military force IRA Volunteers, and/or Republicans. Anti-Treaty Republicans enjoyed direct continuity with the Irish Volunteer organisation founded in 1913; that organisation became popularly known as the Irish Republican Army (IRA) in 1919, after it pledged allegiance to Dáil Éireann and placed itself under the control of the Dáil minister for defence. Between 1919 and 1921, the Volunteer (or IRA) organisation was led by its General Headquarters Staff (which included Richard Mulcahy and Michael Collins), elected originally by a Volunteer convention in 1917. No Volunteer convention met between 1918 and 1921, and overall control of the IRA/Volunteer organisation remained a contested and nebulous issue. After the ratification of the Anglo-Irish Treaty in 1922, a National Army was formed from pro-Treaty IRA units and other recruits who pledged allegiance to the Irish Free State. This set the stage for the IRA convention of March 1922, where Irish Volunteer organisation delegates voted to elect a new governing executive and to withdraw their allegiance to Dáil Éireann. Members of this organisation retained the title of Volunteer, and promised to defend the Irish Republic that had been declared in 1916. When describing these people or their IRA organisation, I deliberately avoid terms such as Executive Forces, Irregulars, anti-Treaty IRA or Mutineers.

Correspondingly, I describe their military opponents as the Free State Army, National Army, National troops or National soldiers. These combatants were full-time soldiers, paid by the Provisional Government of the Irish Free State, which was a non-Republican dominion of the British crown. Since the Irish Free State was not a republic, I do not refer to its officials or supporters as Republicans. I understand the implications and limitations of terms such as invade, attack, assault, defend and liberate.

Some confusion may arise as a result of Cork's status as both a city and a county. For the purposes of this book, Cork is used to mean the city of Cork; when the county is intended, I use County Cork.

*The Battle for Cork* relies on three prominent histories of the Irish Civil War. More than twenty years after its publication, Michael Hopkinson's *Green Against Green: the Irish Civil War* remains the authoritative work on the subject. Hopkinson builds on the work of two earlier Civil War historians, Calton Younger and Eoin Neeson. While preparing *Ireland's Civil War*, Younger conducted extensive interviews with Free State Army leaders, most notably General Emmet Dalton and Commandant Frank O'Friel. For *The Civil War in Ireland*, Cork native Eoin Neeson met surviving Civil War IRA officers in the city, many of whom knew Neeson's parents from joint service in the Republican movement. From the different conversations of Younger and Neeson, a discernible narrative emerges that encompasses both sides of the firing line.

I also drew on Gerry White and Dan Harvey's valuable *The*

*Barracks: A History of Victoria/Collins Barracks, Cork.* Another Cork authority, Colman O'Mahony, provided excellent material from his book, *The Maritime Gateway to Cork: A History of the Outports of Passage West and Monkstown, 1754–1942.* In the course of his research, O'Mahony interviewed a surviving member of the IRA garrison at Passage West, who provided insights regarding the landing of National troops there. Finally, I would be remiss if I did not acknowledge Anne Dolan and Cormac O'Malley's *'No Surrender Here!': The Civil War Papers of Ernie O'Malley.* This exhaustive and well-organised work serves as an essential reference source for IRA communications in 1922.

Readers will note the frequent mentions of Dr James Lynch's first-hand account, 'The Battle of Douglas'. As verified by the 1911 Census, Dr Lynch lived in the area of Douglas/Rochestown that saw the most severe fighting of the battle. His participation as a National Army medical officer was noted in *The Cork Examiner*, and many of the details in his narrative match different newspaper accounts. Lynch provides the best eyewitness testimony of the battle. Newspapers also provided information about the engagement, with *The Cork Examiner* offering first-hand accounts from its reporters on the scene. The *Irish Independent* printed another eyewitness report from a journalist in the city during the three critical days. Correspondents from *The Freeman's Journal* and *The Irish Times* accompanied the invading National Army forces. Photographer W. D. Hogan also travelled with the Free State assault troops, and his pictures frequently verify newspaper details.

# FOREWORD

'How did a city so closely identified with militant Irish republicanism from 1917 to 1921 so easily pass into the hands of the Irish Free State?'

This is the central question posed by the author John Borgonovo in his introduction to this, the latest volume in Mercier Press' *Military History of the Irish Civil War* series. It is a deceptively simple question, to which, as will become apparent, there is no single, or simple, answer. Social stratification certainly played a part, with religion, social class, gender and age all playing their respective roles, as did a variety of human qualities: bravado, courage, fear and, not least, luck.

There were, however, two over-arching and interrelated factors that together effectively determined the outcome. The first was that elusive quality of generalship – the effective direction of forces in combat. The second was that this engagement was indeed a battle – small in scale admittedly, but recognisably an instance of conventional warfare in an area of the country with greater recent experience of, and topographically suited to, guerrilla tactics. The author makes a very convincing case that in this confrontation the driving force behind the Free State attack on the city, Emmet Dalton, handled the resources at his disposal far more competently than did his opposite number Mick Leahy, who, in theory, had the easier task of organising a defence. That defence was not helped, of course, by the utterly inadequate number of men and amount of material under Leahy's control – but this is where the second key issue comes into play, for to hold ground and engage in a set-piece firefight under such circumstances was, with the benefit of hindsight, decidedly unwise.

It is important to bear in mind that while the city of Cork itself fell with scarcely a shot being fired in anger, and with most of the city's buildings, industry and infrastructure intact, the precipitate flight of Republicans to the west of the county followed a battle that, in scale, exceeded the famous victories registered in the county during the Anglo-Irish War, such as Kilmichael and Crossbarry. The fight for Rochestown/Douglas was fought over three days, with dozens of dead and wounded – yet knowledge (or at least discussion) of this is today scarce, even in the locality itself. This is all the more noteworthy given that battle was joined following not just one of the most daring manoeuvres of the entire war, but one of the most difficult of all military actions – the amphibious assault of Free State forces on the IRA-held port facilities in Passage West. Even if the scale was vastly different, the then recent debacle at Gallipoli had shown just how fraught with danger such an opposed landing could be. In skilfully planning and successfully executing this operation, as well as in their conduct during the subsequent engagement on the road into the city, Dalton and his troops more than earned the sycophantic adulation (amongst other forms of attention) showered on them following their ensuing triumphant entry into the city proper.

In conclusion one must remember, of course, that the fall of the city was by no means the end of the fight in County Cork, and the book's coda – the death of Michael Collins at Béal na mBláth in west Cork on 22 August – in many respects signals the start of the second, longer-lasting and more vicious phase of the Civil War in the country as a whole, which was marked by a return to unconventional warfare by Republicans in their Munster fastnesses. In this respect there is a striking symmetry in the local arcs of hostilities in the months and years following the 1916 Rising and the outbreak of the Civil War in 1922. On both occasions Republicans in the city, led initially by MacCurtain and MacSwiney and subsequently by Leahy, for sound military reasons, either refused or felt themselves unable to give conventional battle. In both cases this apparently defeatist passivity was followed by an intense period of guerrilla warfare, albeit one that lasted for a shorter time and was attended with much less success during the latter period. Perhaps – and this can only be a supposition, for we are dealing here with psychological factors not easily verified by the standards of conventional historical investigation – it might be posited that the shameful memory of the one was one of the many causes of the other?

Gabriel Doherty
*Department of History*
*University College Cork*

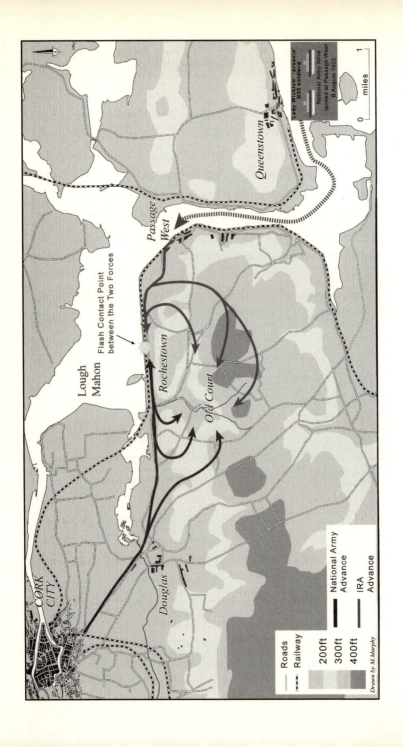

CORK CITY

Lough
Mahon

Passage
West

Queenstown

Flash Contact Point
between the Two Forces

Rochestown

Old Court

Douglas

*Lady Wicklow* 'Arvonia'
450 soldiers

National Army force
landed at Passage West
8 August 1922

0       miles       1

Roads
Railway
200ft
300ft
400ft
National Army
Advance
IRA
Advance

*Drawn by M. Murphy*

# Introduction

Following Dáil Éireann's approval of the Anglo-Irish Treaty on 7 January 1922, the fear of civil war grew throughout Ireland. The Irish Republican Army (IRA) gradually split into pro- and anti-Treaty factions, as its powerful provincial commanders demanded the right to sanction the settlement. After weeks of delays, the Dáil Éireann cabinet (ruling in tandem with the Free State Provisional Government) approved an IRA convention in Dublin, but fearing a *coup d'état*, the Minister for Defence, Richard Mulcahy, promptly reversed his decision, banned the convention and announced the dismissal of any IRA attendee. Despite Mulcahy's threats, the convention opened as scheduled on 26 March 1922, and 223 delegates gathered at the Mansion House, representing a strong majority of IRA brigades and battalions, though anti-Treaty officers suspected the government would attempt to arrest delegates *en masse*. In defying the government ban, they had essentially repudiated their fealty to the civilian authority.

The Cork No. 1 Brigade contingent took no chances, arriving at the Mansion House in their 'bloody big armoured car', 'The River Lee', a massive home-made contraption described as 'a labourer's cottage' on wheels.[1] Wearing trench coats, leggings, collars and ties, the Corkmen filed into the hall past crowds of onlookers, led by their brigade commander, Seán O'Hegarty. Inside, they greeted their cousins from the other Cork brigades, representing the most powerful fighting formations in the independence movement. They sat with the taciturn 1st Southern Division commanders, Florrie O'Donoghue (Cork City), Liam Deasy (West

Cork) and Liam Lynch (North Cork), who controlled the IRA in Cork, Kerry and Waterford. The 1st Southern had enough firepower and experience to launch a civil war by itself, if it so decided.

During the convention proceedings, a series of young speakers denounced Ireland's new status as a dominion of the British Empire. They urged the army to repudiate the Dáil for voting to disestablish the Irish Republic, which the IRA Volunteers had vowed to defend. A vocal faction proposed the immediate creation of an IRA military government to defeat the Treaty. Despite a hard-line reputation, the 1st Southern officers opposed this proposed dictatorship, and their truculent spokesman Seán O'Hegarty eviscerated its advocates. However, the Munster men supported the convention's establishment of an independent Army Executive to govern the IRA. Going forward, the IRA would only answer to its own Volunteers and not the Irish parliament. A clash with the new Free State Provisional Government now seemed possible.

Though the anti-Treaty IRA units enjoyed a strong numeric superiority over the budding National (Free State) Army, they were heavily outgunned. Driving back to Cork city, Republican officers discussed their plan to redress the arms imbalance. Three days later, they launched a naval operation that violated spectacularly the nine-month Truce between the IRA and the crown forces. As the British police and military left Ireland, they had deposited assorted small arms at the Haulbowline naval base in Cork Harbour. At the end of the month, tons of rifles, pistols, ammunition, machine guns and explosives would be transported back to Britain aboard the ordnance steamer *Upnor*. Unfortunately for the Royal Navy, a Republican shipyard worker gained access to the *Upnor*'s manifest and notified the Cork No. 1 Brigade of her scheduled departure. As with many of the Cork City IRA's sallies against the British, the plan was audacious, well-organised and coolly executed.[2]

British coastal forts commanded the mouth of Cork Harbour, while a fleet of Royal Navy warships regularly patrolled the shipping channels. The *Upnor*, therefore, could only be intercepted in the open ocean. Cobh IRA Volunteers gathered a crew of Republican sailors (abundant in a port town), while the City IRA provided the boarding party. On the morning of the operation (2 April 1922), Cobh Republicans approached the Royal Navy headquarters and stole the Admiralty ensign from its mast. They also secured a large brown envelope, similar to those used for carrying official naval communiqués. The Republicans had selected a tug for the operation, but to their chagrin they discovered its absence from its mooring because of engine trouble. On the quays, despondent IRA Volunteers watched the *Upnor* push out of the harbour, before they noticed the docked deep-water tug, *Viking*. They lost valuable time in locating and abducting the *Viking*'s skipper (to prevent him from notifying the naval authorities) and replacing him with veteran shipmaster and Republican sympathiser, Captain Jeremiah Collins. By the time the *Viking* got under way with twenty Republicans on board, they were almost two hours behind their quarry. As the *Viking* steamed out of the harbour at maximum speed, it passed unsuspected beneath British coastal artillery.

In the Celtic Sea a few hours later, the *Upnor* was sighted in the twilight. Closing the distance, the *Viking* hoisted the stolen Admiralty ensign, while the IRA Volunteers hid below deck. A lone Republican crew member waved the giant envelope, signalling an urgent message from naval headquarters. The *Upnor* cut its engines and waited for the *Viking* to pull alongside. The ship sent a launch over to the *Viking*, which was boarded by four armed Republicans, one of whom carried a Thompson machine gun under his trench coat. They motored back to the *Upnor*, climbed aboard, produced their weapons and announced that they were seizing the ship. 'This is piracy on the high seas and it is a hanging matter,' spluttered the captain, a quotation that became enshrined in Republican folklore.[3] The two vessels adjusted course, opened their engines and sped to the small port of Ballycotton, located about twenty miles east of Cork city.

On land, the Cork No. 1 Brigade had not been idle. That morning, Cork Republicans methodically visited garages and commercial premises across the city, seizing almost every available lorry and large car. Armed two-man Volunteer teams drove nearly 100 vehicles to Ballycotton Pier. Other IRA parties blocked roads, cut telephone and telegraph wires, and established outposts around the sleepy coastal town. Volunteers seized the coastguard's wireless station at Roche's Point to intercept naval messages relating to the *Upnor*. All told, nearly 300 Volunteers were involved in the complex amphibious operation. By evening, the reception preparations were complete, though there was still no sign of the *Upnor*. At 4 a.m. Volunteers dozing on the pier were awoken by the sound of engines, and cheering erupted as the two vessels entered the harbour. Once the boats had docked, brigade leaders looked eagerly at their haul, and could hardly believe the deadly bounty they had gained to fight the British Empire.

All through the morning and afternoon, the Republicans off-loaded the weaponry, expecting at any minute to be interrupted by the British. Yet their luck held, as lorry after packed lorry departed for prepared arms dugouts around the county. At midday, the IRA Volunteers had a shock as a warship searching for the *Upnor* cruised past the harbour, but the warship's crew failed to see the off-loading proceeding at the pier. The last vehicles pulled out of the town at sunset, just as the Royal Navy sloop HMS *Heather* docked.[4] The sailors checking the *Upnor* found only broken packing boxes and the ship's inebriated captain. The Republicans had invited him ashore for a meal and drinks, and they had parted on the friendliest of terms, with the captain calling them 'grand fellows'.[5]

In the House of Commons, the embarrassed colonial secretary, Winston Churchill, denounced 'the gang of Republican conspirators', who 'piratically seized' the *Upnor* on the high seas. He also pointed out to the Free State Provisional Government, 'their control over Cork and this district is practically non-existent'.[6] Back in Cork, the IRA distributed 400 rifles, almost doubling the 1st Southern Division's supply, as well as hundreds of thousands of rounds of precious .303 ammunition, and at least forty machine guns. Brigade engineers eyed greedily numerous crates of high explosives. Having recently mastered the production of landmines, they finally had the means to mass produce them.

Overnight, the Cork No. 1 Brigade had upgraded its firepower dramatically and could meet the British-armed National Army on something like equal terms. For the Free State authorities to secure a lasting settlement between Britain and Ireland, they now needed either to win the Corkmen's approval or to beat them into submission. Republican Cork prepared for both contingencies.

# CHAPTER 1

# THE TREATY DEBATE IN CORK

By late 1921, 'Rebel Cork' was a city synonymous with militant Republicanism. It had earned an international reputation as a result of the assassination of Lord Mayor Tomás MacCurtain and the hunger strike of his successor, Terence MacSwiney, both of whom had commanded the Cork No. 1 Brigade, IRA. Further notoriety followed the burning of the city centre by crown forces in December 1920. IRA street fighters punched back with assassinations, ambushes and executions of suspected informers, keeping residents on edge. The city acted as a fulcrum for Republican resistance across County Cork, serving as an intelligence and communications conduit to the Cork No. 2 and Cork No. 3 Brigades in north and west Cork. Together, these three Cork brigades faced a disproportionate number of British troops in Ireland, and mustered the IRA's most sophisticated and lethal guerrilla organisation.

## THE ANGLO-IRISH TREATY
The Truce of July 1921 seems to have been arranged with little input from provincial IRA units in Cork or elsewhere. IRA Volunteers throughout the 1st Southern Division welcomed the break, though senior officers believed their organisation was gaining strength when hostilities were suspended. From their perspective, they had defeated the British, which made the Anglo-Irish Treaty signed in December 1921 all the more shocking.

The Anglo-Irish Treaty disestablished the Irish Republic declared by Dáil Éireann in January 1919. Southern Ireland became a self-governing dominion within the British Empire, headed by the king of England. Republicans objected to continued citizenship within the empire, enshrined in an oath of allegiance to the king. The endorsement of a partitioned Northern Ireland state only added to the distaste for the settlement. Pragmatists argued that the Treaty provided most elements of political independence and the potential to achieve the difference in future years. More important, the alternative was renewed war with the British Empire, the world's reigning superpower at that time. To Treaty supporters, Ireland was dancing on a razor's edge between independence and annihilation.

Contemporary perspectives of the Irish Civil War assume a slow build-up to an inevitable clash between pro- and anti-Treaty supporters. However, events often moved with bewildering speed, as new developments reset the situation every month or so. The Treaty was signed on 5 December and the Dáil debates began a week later. On 14 January 1922, the Dáil ratified the Treaty and established the Provisional Government; the British evacuation began immediately. During February and March, IRA provincial leaders resisted the Treaty, and by April they had repudiated the Dáil and occupied the Four Courts in Dublin. In May Republican peace negotiations pointed towards a resolution and by early June de Valera and Collins had produced their Election Pact to rule the country through a coalition government, with the army being commanded by officers from both sides of the Treaty divide. Two weeks after the election, Provisional Government forces bombarded the Four Courts. Initial hope that the war could be confined to Dublin disappeared immediately, as fighting erupted across the country.

Events in Cork broadly followed the national trajectory, with some notable exceptions. A Republican front composed of the IRA, Sinn Féin, Cumann na mBan and the Cork Labour Party had effectively ruled the city since early 1920. When the Anglo-Irish Treaty negotiations began in London, Cork Republicans watched from the sidelines, learning new details from the intense newspaper coverage.

Remarkably, though the Irish cabinet anticipated something short of a Republican settlement (including de Valera's preferred 'external association'), politicians made little effort to prepare the IRA for a compromise. Visiting Cork in October 1921, just before he left for London, Michael Collins addressed the Munster IRA's senior leadership, under the auspices of the Irish Republican Brotherhood (IRB). Before his speech, he casually mentioned to Liam Lynch, Florrie O'Donoghue and a couple of others that he thought a non-Republican agreement might be signed, which O'Donoghue recalled was, 'the first indication that any of these officers heard' of such a possibility. Collins then informed the larger assembly that they would be consulted before any agreement was concluded. In November and December, the Cork IRB repeatedly asked the IRB Supreme Council (headed by Collins) for clarification about the direction the talks had taken, but heard nothing. The announcement of non-Republican Treaty terms therefore shocked the Cork IRA.[1]

Cork's conservative political elements immediately welcomed the settlement. The Redmondite *Cork Examiner* wrote celebratory editorials for a week, announcing 'Ireland's Triumph', and claiming 'reason has triumphed over force'.[2] Cardinal Logue and the Irish bishops championed the Treaty terms, with Cork bishop, Daniel Cohalan, scheduling masses of thanksgiving across the diocese.[3] (Cohalan had excommunicated IRA fighters in 1920.) The Cork

Chamber of Commerce laid out signature books for business leaders to record their support, while Redmondite politicians spoke in its favour.[4] Constitutionalist bodies such as the South of Ireland Cattle-traders and the Cork Legion of Ex-Servicemen similarly endorsed the agreement.[5] The day the Treaty terms were published, the British government released thousands of Irish prisoners, adding to an end-of-war atmosphere. Hundreds of Cork Volunteers returned home to celebratory welcomes, as detention camps at Bere Island, Spike Island and Ballykinlar were emptied.[6] Because of the optimistic coverage in the pro-Treaty Cork newspapers, it took the public a few days to realise the depth of Republican hostility to the Treaty.

On 10 December, the powerful 1st Southern Division informed IRA General Headquarters (GHQ) that its officers opposed the Treaty.[7] Cork No. 1 Brigade commander Seán O'Hegarty told the city's two pro-Treaty members of the Irish parliament (TDs) that he considered a 'yes' vote to be 'treason to the Republic', a fatal offence in Cork.[8] During the Dáil debates, the IRA obstructed pro-Treaty lobbying, destroying pamphlets and confiscating Chamber of Commerce signature books.[9] When city Sinn Féin clubs gathered to elect delegates to the party's pivotal Ard Fheis, IRA Volunteers packed the meetings to elect anti-Treaty representatives. At one branch meeting, IRA leader Dan 'Sandow' O'Donovan reportedly secured his election by warning that no pro-Treaty delegate 'would leave Cork alive'.[10]

Seán O'Hegarty's belligerence towards the press had already made international headlines at the end of December 1921. Writing from Cork, *Times* correspondent A. B. Kay claimed that local IRA officers supported the Treaty and opposed resuming hostilities with Britain. Warned of Republican anger about his article, Kay fled Cork, but IRA intelligence promptly tracked him to a Dublin hotel. While Kay sipped tea with fellow international journalists, Cork City IRA commanders Sandow O'Donovan and Mick Murphy entered the Dublin café. Both the armed men were prominent Gaelic Athletic Association (GAA) athletes and they had no difficulty in bundling Kay into a waiting Rolls-Royce sedan driven by Jim Grey. In style, they rode all night to a lonely cottage a few miles from Cork. The following evening Seán O'Hegarty convened a brigade court-martial which convicted Kay of delibe- rately distorting the IRA position. Forced to choose between deportation and publishing a correction, Kay opted for the latter and was released unharmed. When he was dropped in Cork city, Kay found Michael Collins' GHQ officers frantically searching for him, in an attempt to head off an international incident. Kay wrote fondly of his Cork captors, who took him for strolls in the countryside, bought him drinks and shared their bed with him. This widely reported incident did nothing to diminish Cork's rep- utation for fierce unilateral action.[11]

In this volatile political situation, Cork's public bodies largely abstained from the Treaty debates. Cork's Harbour Commission, Poor Law Guardians, Cork Trades Council and Rural District Council refused to offer an opinion on the matter. 'What we want to preserve in Ireland at all costs is unity,' explained Harbour Com- missioner Frank Daly.[12] Cork labour officials called for a 'Worker's Republic' and a plebiscite to decide the Treaty issue, but expressed no specific constitutional preference. Appealing for national unity, Cork Corporation specifically refused to vote on the Treaty itself; only the County Council recorded its opinion, supporting the Treaty on a narrow vote of fifteen to fourteen. Public bodies seem- ingly feared that their intervention might derail internal Sinn Féin deliberations and inadvertently trigger a violent split.[13]

The Dáil's Treaty vote on Saturday 7 January aroused tremen- dous interest in the city. Throughout the afternoon and evening, large crowds gathered outside the *Examiner* newspaper office awaiting the verdict from Dublin. When the result was finally chalked onto headline boards, some in the crowd cheered while others rushed off to spread the word. Local cinema audiences learned of the vote from special bulletin slides inserted into the films. At a pantomime in the Cork Opera House, the battling puppets 'Iky' and 'Will Scott' delivered the news to the audience, and then shook hands to signify lasting peace between the old enemies of England and Ireland.[14]

Within hours of the Treaty's passage, the crown forces in Cork began their evacuation, adding to the momentum. Optimism, however, disappeared two days later, when the Cork No. 1 Brigade forced the *Examiner* to run a large advertisement that explained its stance in no uncertain terms:

> The Irish Republic still lives. No 'Free State' government will take place; no 'Free State' Army will be formed in the south of Ireland; no 'Free State' judiciary will ever function without determined opposition. The Irish Republican Army fought that the Republic might live. It shall continue to live.[15]

Throughout its eight-year existence, the IRA had governed itself democratically, characterised by elected leaders and collective decision-making. Despite raising hundreds of thousands of pounds during the 1919–21 war, Dáil Éireann provided the IRA with little direct support; units raised their own funds, armed themselves and were essentially unpaid. The Dáil only assumed responsibility for IRA actions in the final stage of the War of Independence. This contributed to the army's independent outlook and decentralised structure. In turn, provincial IRA officers were highly critical of the GHQ staff in Dublin, who failed to secure weapons for pressed units, despite the abundance of these in post-war Europe. Thus the settlement's endorsement by army leaders Michael Collins, Richard Mulcahy and their (non-elected) GHQ staff failed to sway the rest of the army, despite government assumptions to the contrary. Collins and his colleagues presented the Treaty to the IRA membership as a *fait accompli*, naïvely assuming unquestioning obedience. They underestimated the IRA rank-and-file's commitment to their role as guardians of an Irish Republic they had secured by force of arms. To these IRA Volunteers, no single leader, ruling clique or governing group had the right to hand over that Republic of its own volition. IRA officers in Munster remained incredulous that they were not consulted before the Treaty was submitted for ratification. Writing in 1929, Florrie O'Donoghue expressed this militarist view:

> The Army created Sinn Féin in the country; the Army created and controlled every national activity from 1916 to the truce of 1921. The Army was the deciding factor in the 1918 elections; it made and largely manned the Dáil and the Government of the Republic. The Army put the Dáil in power and kept it there; it directed and controlled every department of that government. The Army policy was the policy of the government, everything else was subservient to it; it was the driving force of the whole movement for independence. To misunderstand this would be to misunderstand the whole position of the Army.[16]

## THE GROWING SPLIT

Facing what it considered to be an anti-Republican conspiracy, the Cork IRA attempted to stymie rapid implementation of the Treaty. Their politicking aroused the ire of pro-Treaty politicians such as TD J. J. Walsh, who protested in a public letter to Irish newspapers that IRA Volunteers had been ordered to canvass for public support, and 'assumed the role of an armed political junta'. Walsh urged the citizens to 'trust the fortunes of their country to two or three men': Michael Collins, Richard Mulcahy and Arthur Griffith. Seán O'Hegarty responded by forcing local newspapers to run an edited version of Walsh's letter that omitted 'internal army matters', and destroyed copies of Dublin newspapers that ran the full item.[17]

Despite IRA opposition, a pro-Treaty consensus emerged in Cork. Immediate support came from political bodies already at odds with the Republicans. With few exceptions, constitutional nationalists in the Irish Party, All-for-Ireland League (AFIL) and British ex-servicemen's associations endorsed the Treaty. Unionists, including many of the city's 'merchant princes', also threw their weight behind the Provisional Government. With this strong foundation, pro-Treaty Republicans (as they still considered themselves) built up a powerful coalition in the city.

The lower-middle-class leadership of Cork's Sinn Féin party also largely supported the Treaty. Many of these politicians had been squeezed out of the Irish Volunteers because of their reluctance to fight in the Easter Rising.[18] Cork's first two Republican TDs, Liam de Róiste and J. J. Walsh, acted as vocal and visible supporters of the settlement. Though respectable, these political leaders retained little influence over the IRA and its second generation of young, working-class officers. The IRA's lower social status can be seen in the 1st Southern Division's leadership triumvirate: Liam Deasy was a carpenter; Florrie O'Donoghue, a draper's shop assistant; and Liam Lynch, a hardware shop assistant. Some of the subsequent hostility towards the IRA in Cork can be attributed to class resentment about 'high-handed' Republican officers rising above their perceived station.

A more surprising Republican defection occurred when a majority of Cork's Cumann na mBan branches supported the Treaty.[19] The organisation was closely associated with Mary Mac-Swiney, one of the most hard-line opponents of the Treaty. Yet,

MacSwiney was a highly controversial character within the Cork Cumann na mBan. She had been at the heart of a destructive split in the Cork organisation, which at one point in 1918 saw two parallel Cumann na mBan organisations in the city. Though ousted from the Cork leadership, Mary MacSwiney directed its national executive to expel five of her Cork opponents, causing bad blood between Dublin and Cork for three years. Effectively two wings of the organisation operated in Cork, with the majority strongly opposed to MacSwiney. Voting on the Treaty, the city branches accepted it by a majority of eight branches to four. Afterwards, Cork's Cumann na mBan leadership largely endorsed the Treaty, though much of the organisation's rank and file supported the IRA during the August fighting.[20] Overall, the split critically damaged the Cork Cumann na mBan, and neither wing of the organisation proved to be as effective in the Civil War as it had been in the War of Independence.

Cork's Labour Party took a neutral stance on the entire question of the Treaty. It had been the junior member of the city's Republican front, having abstained from the 1918 general election, and run a joint ticket with Sinn Féin in the 1920 local elections. Labour saw abstract constitutional questions as a distraction from a pending European class war and the post-war depression in Ireland. To the Irish Transport and General Workers' Union (ITGWU) and the Cork Trades Council, bread-and-butter issues trumped questions of association with the British Empire. Labour essentially withdrew from the subsequent national split, which helped the pro-Treaty forces.

The final element of the Cork independence movement was the IRA, which strongly opposed the Treaty. The Cork No. 1 Brigade enjoyed a reputation for independent action, and its leaders played a forceful role in IRA convention debates. Within the city of Cork, the brigades fielded two battalions numbering about 2,200 members, which were organised into sixteen companies. Fifteen of the sixteen companies opposed the Treaty. The single exception was C Company, 1st Battalion, (centred on Blarney Street) which had suffered heavy casualties in the Anglo-Irish War. About 100 of its members enlisted in the new Free State Army, joining some 500 other Volunteers from around County Cork. Liam de Róiste also reported a steady stream of applicants for the new Irish police force, an attractive alternative during a period of high unemployment. Outside the city, the remaining eight Cork No. 1 Brigade battalions stretched from east to west across the middle of Cork. These units all opposed the Treaty, with the exception of the 10th Youghal Battalion and a 3rd Battalion faction centred on Midleton. The latter's senior officers had been court-martialled for robbery, and they organised a pro-Treaty group in east Cork. But such dissidents were a minority in mid-Cork. Overall, the Cork No. 1 Brigade could field scores of experienced guerrilla fighters and a few thousand support personnel strongly opposed to the Treaty.[21]

## GAUGING PUBLIC OPINION

Weeks after the Treaty's passage, the Cork IRA turned out in force to greet Éamon de Valera during a mass meeting on the Grand Parade. A motion denounced the Treaty as 'an agreement obtained under duress', claiming it was non-binding, unless 'the Irish people of their own free will disestablished the Republic'. The large turnout was thanked by de Valera: 'There was one city in Ireland that knew what it was doing.'[22] At this stage, the local IRA Volunteers seemed to believe they still enjoyed public support and that their threats could peacefully rebuff implementation of the Treaty. Ominously, de Valera's rally generated little public enthusiasm.

Republican delusions disappeared when Michael Collins arrived in Cork for a mass meeting in favour of the agreement on 13 March

1922.[23] Up to 50,000 people attended the huge gathering, among the largest in the city's history. Collins promised jobs for the city and reconstruction funds, and shouted, 'there is no mistaking the attitude of Cork city'. (He subsequently granted £250,000 in government reconstruction aid to the city, and another £112,000 for housing assistance.)[24] Collins' two-day visit produced high tension and IRA harassment of the pro-Treaty party. Before he arrived, Collins' speaking platform was destroyed by Republican men and women, who left a sign reading 'Surrender'. Armed Republicans blocked a marching band on its way to the meeting and tossed a bass drum into the river. More dangerously, during the speeches a senior Cork No. 1 Brigade officer positioned in front of the platform fired shots into the air to scatter the crowd, until bystanders disarmed him. However, the audience bravely stood its ground and the meeting continued. Afterwards, Michael Collins, Seán MacEoin of Longford and pro-Treaty politicians attempted to lay a wreath at the Republican Plot in Cork's St Finbarr's Cemetery. When they arrived, an IRA patrol blocked them at the gate, drew pistols and threatened to fire if they entered. Seán MacEoin started to reply in kind, before Collins led the party away from the showdown. At a concert in his honour that night, more shots were fired in the hall and red pepper powder was blown across the crowd. Liam de Róiste believed the local Republicans 'have decided to create disorder and terror'.[25]

This episode proved to be the high-water mark of anti-Treaty intimidation. Before Collins' visit, Cork Republicans had had the luxury of blaming the passage of the Treaty on political enemies who had not supported them during the War of Independence: the commercial elite, the newspapers, Redmondites, ex-soldiers and the Catholic Church. Yet the city's rapturous reception for Michael Collins clearly demonstrated the mass of public opinion was opposed to renewed hostilities with Britain. Many demanded a resumption of peace after eight years of political turmoil that included the Home Rule crisis, the First World War, the Easter Rising, the Conscription crisis and the War of Independence. This reality seemed to have struck Cork No. 1 Brigade commander Seán O'Hegarty in particular. Over the coming weeks, he and his Cork officers showed little appetite for creating an IRA dictatorship or for starting a civil war for which they had little public support. Only three options lay open to Cork Republicans: to secure a compromise with their pro-Treaty opponents that satisfied their principles; to re-launch the war with the British to unify the country; or to physically resist the Free State to inspire the public, as the Easter Rising had done six years earlier. None of these tasks would be easy.

# CHAPTER 2

# THE ROAD TO CIVIL WAR

Following the Dáil's ratification of the Treaty on 14 January 1922, British forces immediately started to evacuate southern Ireland. Auxiliary cadets stationed in Macroom began the British withdrawal on 14 January, and the entire force was gone a week later. Departing British troops handed over certain barracks to the IRA in late January. The Royal Irish Constabulary (RIC) started to demobilise at the beginning of February, leaving law enforcement to the IRA police. The crown forces' rapid evacuation created a power vacuum in the country: the Provisional Government was just beginning to organise itself; the state's constitutional status was an open question; there was no government police force; Republicans opposed the new government; and the IRA itself was a volunteer force with few full-time members. Without a governing authority, the situation became increasingly chaotic as social divisions erupted.[1]

## GROWING ANARCHY

Cork experienced destabilising labour agitation throughout the period from January to June 1922. Irish trade unionism was at a high-water mark, led by the socialist ITGWU. Amid a debilitating post-war recession and high unemployment, attempts by employers to reduce wages created industrial strife. Within days of the establishment of the Provisional Government, a national railway strike paralysed the Irish economy.

In Cork, hundreds of workers downed tools, shutting the Munster railway network in late January 1922. The stoppage continued for three weeks, closing the Port of Cork and crippling trade. Cork's Industrial Co-operative Strike Committee prepared to seize and run the railway network as a soviet, in a plan they dubbed 'Document Number Two'. A union leader promised, 'The railways would now be operated by the workers, for the workers and under the control of the workers.' On 10 February, over 700 strikers marched in military formation to the city's five railway terminals. Large crowds watched the workers expel staff, occupy offices and post guards outside all the premises; the union leaders planned to run the trains themselves the following day. Fortunately for Munster's railway directors, a national wage settlement was reached the same day and Dublin officials successfully ended the Cork occupation.[2] Though it ended peacefully, the strike demonstrated worker power that echoed Bolshevik Russia.[3]

More radical strikes occurred among flour and dairy labourers in north Cork, Tipperary and Limerick.[4] In February, Dáil Éireann ordered anti-Treaty IRA units to help end worker occupations of flour factories in Mallow and Fermoy.[5] During May, workers seized creameries in multiple locations, declared soviets and in some cases flew the red flag. The Cork Chamber of Commerce demanded government intervention, while the Irish Farmers' Union warned that the strikes were 'the thin wedge of Bolshevism'.[6] Serious unrest also erupted in Cork's 'liberties' (now suburban Cork), among the ITGWU's farm labourers.[7] In April, 800 workers went on strike for three weeks, targeting local milk suppliers. They attacked dairy vehicles and drivers, cut communications and blocked roads. The city's merchant classes watched uneasily as ITGWU leaders urged 'workers, arise to action', promising 'all privileges of wealth and birth shall be abolished'.[8]

Additional unrest resulted from the collapse of policing following the RIC's departure. The new Civic Guard (an Garda Síochána) was not yet established, and part-time IRA police (IRAP) struggled to cope. Land-grabbing became endemic, along with cattle-drives, larceny and armed robberies.[9] The city experienced frequent burglaries, vehicle thefts and assaults, especially in April and May.[10] Personal scores were settled and mercenary criminals enjoyed an open field. The IRAP made multiple arrests, but it fielded only a fraction of the strength of the old RIC. The IRA's covert nature made matters worse, since thieves frequently claimed to be acting on its behalf. Sometimes the Cork IRA charged fellow Volunteers with criminal acts such as car theft;[11] but unaffiliated criminals were also caught impersonating the IRA.[12] Some preyed on local Unionists and/or Protestants, who were often wealthy and politically isolated. *The Irish Times* reported, 'Southern Unionists and Protestants are special sufferers from the present conditions of lawlessness', which caused them to fear for their safety.[13]

Though Cork Protestants largely escaped the 1920–1 conflict intact, the spectre of religious war hovered over Munster in 1922. In the first half of that year, savage sectarian violence struck Ulster, and it seemed possible that the province's Catholic population might be expelled. This left Cork Protestants vulnerable to possible IRA retaliation. In early April, Cork's leading Protestant merchants publicly denounced anti-Catholic violence in Northern Ireland, but were careful to point out, 'We have not been subjected to any form of oppression or injustice by our Catholic fellow citizens.'[14]

Fear increased at the end of April, following the brutal assassination of ten Protestants in the Bandon Valley. Over three consecutive nights, unknown IRA gunmen visited at least a dozen homes on their own list of Unionist enemies.[15] The unauthorised killings drove out at least 100 Cork Protestants, with many passing through the city as they fled. Public bodies throughout the city and county condemned the killings, as did Catholic and Protestant clerics.[16] The situation eased only after IRA leaders vowed to protect local Protestants; especially effective was Cork No. 3 Brigade commander, Tom Hales, who threatened publicly to execute any IRA Volunteers involved in new attacks.[17] City Unionists were further frightened in June, when a delegation of homeless Belfast Catholics asked the Cork Corporation to seize Protestant homes to provide accommodation for the scores of refugees in the city.[18] In these months, sectarian anxiety peaked in Cork, as the county peered into the abyss of religious warfare before slowly backing away.

Gerard Murphy's recent book, *The Year of Disappearances: Political Killings in Cork 1921–1922* argues that Cork Protestants were the target of an IRA killing spree in March, April and May 1922.[19] Murphy's charges of IRA mass murder are unproven and unconvincing. It should be emphasised that these supposed killings are not mentioned in British government, Irish government, Northern Ireland government, IRA, Free State Army, Catholic or Protestant records; the families of these so-called 'disappeared' did not protest or make enquiries about their missing loved ones, nor did they apply for compensation for their deaths. Dozens of people do not disappear without any mention in the public record. As such, Murphy's claims must be discounted without written proof.[20]

Protestant and loyalist families who left Cork during these months did so for a variety of reasons. There was growing political, social and criminal unrest; a deteriorating economy; a new Irish state that might prove to be anti-Protestant; fear that sectarian strife in Belfast would spread to Cork; and anxiety over a pending civil war or British military intervention. Any of these issues on its own would cause a resident to rethink his or her position. Some decided to leave the city temporarily, others permanently, but many more stayed where they were. Each choice was understandable in the turbulent circumstances.

## THE MACROOM DISAPPEARANCES

As the last British troops evacuated Ireland, an incident in Macroom nearly renewed hostilities with Britain. On 27 April 1922, three British army officers and their military driver stopped in Macroom to gather information about local conditions. While they lunched at the Williams Hotel, IRA Volunteers investigated the visitors. Though the officers were not wearing uniforms, the absence of license plates on their car identified them as members of military intelligence. In a clear violation of the Truce, the IRA swooped on the four men and hustled them into Macroom Castle, headquarters of the Cork No. 1 Brigade's 7th Battalion.

Two of the officers, Lt R. A. Hendy and Lt G. R. A. Dove, had been implicated in the torture and unauthorised killing of IRA prisoners. In addition, Republicans accused them of mapping IRA positions in violation of the Truce. Apparently with the approval of Seán O'Hegarty, the Macroom Volunteers secretly shot the four soldiers that night and buried them in a bog at Kilgobnet, seven miles away.[21]

After the officers failed to return to their base, a military search party scoured the area and learned that the men had been taken to Macroom Castle. Over the next three days, British army delegations visited IRA headquarters at Union Quay (Cork) and Macroom Castle to demand their release. The IRA allowed two British officers to search Macroom Castle; unimpressed, the British army suspended its evacuation until the officers were returned. Increasing the pressure, on 30 April a large British army convoy arrived in Macroom commanded by a 17th Brigade staff officer, Major Bernard 'Monty' Montgomery, later to gain fame as a

Second World War field marshal. Montgomery drove into the town square and summoned IRA battalion adjutant Charlie Brown from the castle, but he denied any knowledge of the missing officers. The meeting grew tense when the British trained their guns on the castle and Montgomery threatened reprisals against the town. Worried shopkeepers shuttered their windows, while a Catholic priest tried to calm both sides. Eventually Montgomery withdrew, but vowed to return.

Two days later, he pulled into the Macroom town square with lorries, four armoured cars and sixty men, and demanded admittance to the castle. Charlie Brown again emerged from the castle gates, seemingly covered by a single sniper in a turret, 'showing his rifle against the might of England'. However, this time Brown was in no mood for Montgomery's threats. In front of scores of nervous onlookers, Brown gave Montgomery an ultimatum: the British had ten minutes to leave the square, or else Brown 'wouldn't be responsible for what happened'. Brown turned on his heels and marched back inside the castle gates, ignoring Montgomery's shouts for him to stop. Montgomery did not realise that the Macroom IRA had summoned reinforcements from the Cork No. 1 Brigade's 6th and 8th Battalions. At least 100 Volunteers armed with rifles, machine guns and mines were already posted in houses and fields overlooking the British convoy, which was squeezed into Macroom's narrow streets. One of the armoured cars had even been parked over an IRA landmine. Stepping from a doorway, 8th Battalion commander Pat Lynch whistled at Montgomery and drew his attention to the IRA positions surrounding his force. After assessing the situation briefly, Montgomery swallowed his pride and retreated from the town.

During subsequent debates in the House of Commons this unceremonious withdrawal generated accusations of cowardice, yet Montgomery survived with his life and career intact. The question of how the killing of 'Monty' by the Cork IRA would have affected the outcome of the Second World War is best left to military historians.[22] The British Army resumed its withdrawal from Cork without locating their missing officers, though their fate became known to British officials and to 'everybody who knows anything in Macroom'.[23] The bodies of the four men were eventually recovered in December 1923 and returned to Britain with full military honours by the National Army in Cork. The episode proved to be the Cork IRA's parting insult to the British army, though the Republicans were to suffer their own humiliation at Macroom Castle in due course.

## PEACE EFFORTS

On 24 April, the Irish Labour Party held a one-day general strike to protest 'the spirit of militarism'. The entire country came to a halt, as mass meetings denounced IRA intervention in domestic politics amid continued Republican threats of military dictatorship. In Cork, thousands of workers on the Grand Parade listened to anti-war speeches from a unified trade union movement.[24] During the same week, the Irish bishops issued a stinging condemnation of the Republicans, calling their rejection of civilian authority both 'a sacrilege against national freedom', and 'an immoral usurpation and confiscation of the people's rights'. The bishops declared that 'young men connected with this military revolt are reminded that when, in prosecution of these principles, they make war, they are parricides, not patriots; when they shoot their brothers, murderers; when they injure property, robbers and brigands'.[25]

In the face of increasing public hostility and rising tension with the Free State Army, Cork's moderate anti-Treaty IRA leaders sought to avert civil war. Using the IRB as a starting point, Florrie O'Donoghue and Seán O'Hegarty worked to prevent what they called 'the greatest calamity in Irish history'. Seán O'Hegarty led a group of moderate anti-Treaty officers into the Dáil, and appealed to the chamber for a peace settlement:

> What does civil war mean? To my mind it means not alone that you do not maintain the Republic but that you break for ever any idea of it, that you break the country so utterly and leave it in such a way that England simply walks in and has her way as she never had it before.[26]

Though the IRA Executive repudiated O'Hegarty and O'Donoghue, momentum grew for a compromise. Senior IRA officers searched for a formula that would bring the army back under civilian leadership, despite continued opposition to the efforts from anti-Treaty militants.[27] Previously seen as a major opponent of the Provisional Government, the Cork No. 1 Brigade now emerged as a peace broker, even threatening to stay neutral if hostilities developed. At the end of April, Seán O'Hegarty paraded the city Volunteer companies and announced a new policy. Going forward, the Cork No. 1 Brigade would assume a 'non-political' role, encourage army reunification and support the holding of free elections in June. Though the change was 'an absolute surprise' to hard-line officers, it held the brigade together before the final withdrawal of crown forces from both Cork and Ireland.[28]

As the British prepared to evacuate Cork's Victoria barracks, Michael Collins faced a dilemma. He could order pro-Treaty IRA troops to occupy the barracks, using 100 Volunteers from C Company, 1st Battalion, Cork No. 1 Brigade, under Captain Jeremiah Dennehy. But this could spark anti-Treaty resistance, which would scupper army unification. The other option was to allow Seán O'Hegarty's anti-Treaty forces to assume control of the posts, in the hope that it would be another step towards national unity. Ultimately, Collins chose the latter option and negotiated a settlement with the Cork No. 1 Brigade. The Corkmen would take charge of the barracks and receive government financial support for the garrison's upkeep, and in exchange the brigade promised to support army reunification and not to interfere in the coming election. The Republican garrison at Victoria barracks subsequently received a weekly salary that matched the pay of Free State soldiers at the Curragh. When fifty unemployed former British soldiers heard news of the pay rate, they attempted to join the garrison, but were turned away.[29]

The British evacuation from Cork produced spontaneous celebrations on 18 May 1922. Thousands gathered outside Victoria barracks in the early evening. As the final British vehicles left through the front gates, each brought a cheer from the crowd. At 7 p.m. the last British troops marched from the barracks, having lowered the Union Jack and cut down the flagpole. Captain J. G. Magahy handed the keys to Captain Hugh MacNeill (Eoin Mac-Neill's nephew), representing the Provisional Government, while an IRA advance guard tactfully waited at the rear gate. Passing through applauding crowds, 200 Cork No. 1 Brigade riflemen marched into Victoria barracks behind the IRA pipe band. British control of Cork had officially ended.[30]

The Treaty divide seemed narrower than ever, and it looked as though civil war would be avoided. Within the army, a reunification scheme had finally been negotiated that would split the IRA leadership between pro- and anti-Treaty officers, under a civilian minister for defence approved by an IRA Army Council. Florrie O'Donoghue, tentatively appointed as adjutant general, was optimistic enough to order a Free State Army general's uniform (O'Donoghue never wore the uniform, however, and later donated it to the Cork Public Museum).

Politically, the forthcoming general election yielded an unexpected 'Pact' between Michael Collins and Éamon de Valera. Both

Treaty factions agreed to field a unified Sinn Féin electoral slate; voters would be able to choose Sinn Féin candidates regardless of their stance on the Treaty. Following the election, a coalition government would be formed, with cabinet posts representing both sides of the split. With Michael Collins promising a Republican constitution (the final document was still being written), a peaceful solution seemed to be in the offing.

The June general election went ahead with calm and restraint, but little enthusiasm.[31] In the four-seat Cork city constituency, pro-Treaty Sinn Féin TDs Liam de Róiste and J. J. Walsh were the clear front-runners. The city also fielded two strong commercial candidates: moderate Unionist Richard Beamish (a well-known brewer) and independent, pro-Treaty Sinn Féin merchant Frank Daly, the chairman of the Harbour Commissioners. Labour had unified behind socialist ITGWU leader Bob Day, who called for economic fairness and a plebiscite to approve the Treaty. Observers considered the anti-Treaty Sinn Féin candidates Mary MacSwiney and Lord Mayor Donal Óg O'Callaghan to be highly vulnerable. O'Callaghan had drawn the ire of the ITGWU in frequent clashes over municipal government staffing, and was also viewed warily by Republicans because of his initial ambivalence to the Treaty. The Sinn Féin Pact candidates held one rally in Cork, which drew large crowds and stalwart speakers from both sides of the Treaty divide. De Valera told a large crowd on the Grand Parade, 'Let nobody think they [are] yet out of the woods. They [are] not.'[32] However, Liam de Róiste reported little enthusiasm among Cork's pro-Treaty party for the Pact, and expected that the anti-Treaty party would be strongly defeated.

Polling day produced no violence, and a level of voter fraud that was normal by Cork standards. The Labour Party's Bob Day headed the poll; the previous year he had led the ITGWU's brief Port of Cork workers' soviet. Triumphant union members marched about the city carrying red flags and burning tar barrels. Apparently by pre-arrangement, virtually none of Day's surplus votes went to anti-Treaty Sinn Féin candidates. Anti-Treaty Lord Mayor Donal Óg O'Callaghan was humiliated, finishing last among the major candidates. Labour attributed his defeat to unpopularity among ITGWU voters and a lack of Republican enthusiasm for his candidature. First preference tallies showed a strong pro-Treaty preference:

| | |
|---|---|
| Day | 6,836 |
| Walsh | 5,731 |
| De Róiste | 5,657 |
| MacSwiney | 4,016 |
| Beamish | 3,485 |
| Daly | 2,826 |
| O'Callaghan | 1,796[33] |

While pro-Treaty candidates performed well in the election, three of the four seats went to Sinn Féin's electoral platform calling for a coalition government across the Treaty divide. The big victor, the Labour Party, condemned the pro-Treaty party's release of the new Irish constitution on the day of the election, which prevented voters from passing judgement on that document. 'And this,' howled the *Voice of Labour* newspaper, 'by people who have been prating about "the sovereign people" and "democracy"!'[34]

Despite the optimism arising from the peaceful election, hard realities about the Treaty began to intrude. The newly released constitution merely clarified dominion status under the Treaty terms. Within the IRA, the army was bitterly divided between moderates (led by 1st Southern Division officers) supporting army unification under a pro- and anti-Treaty power-sharing arrangement, and militants (led by Rory O'Connor and Liam Mellows) opposed to any settlement with their pro-Treaty opponents. On 18 June, the militants stormed out of a final IRA convention, locked Liam Lynch and his staff out of the Four Courts headquarters in Dublin, and elected a new chief of staff. Anti-Treaty Republicans now seemed to have a permanent fracture between their moderate and militant wings.[35]

On 22 June, members of the London IRA apparently decided unilaterally to assassinate Field Marshal Sir Henry Wilson, on his own doorstep.[36] The British government incorrectly blamed the killing on Republican militants from the Four Courts, and demanded that the Provisional Government move against them. On 26 June, British Prime Minister David Lloyd George issued an ultimatum: if the Provisional Government refused to remove the militants from the Four Courts, the Treaty would be considered 'formally violated' and the British would have 'liberty of action'. British intervention would be fatal to the Provisional Government. The time seemed to have arrived to eliminate the threat of armed opposition to the Treaty. Since the Four Courts militants had split with the 1st Southern moderates, it was hoped that the fighting could be confined to Dublin. National troops commanded by General Tom Ennis began shelling the Four Courts on the night of 27 June 1922.[37]

Unbeknown to the Provisional Government, during the previous week Liam Lynch and his 1st Southern colleagues had been negotiating a reunification with the Four Courts militants. When the assault began, Lynch assembled a number of senior Republicans and agreed to support the besieged garrison. Lynch and his Cork staff officers promptly returned to their Mallow headquarters to co-ordinate Republican resistance. A communiqué announced that Lynch had resumed his post as IRA chief of staff and his forces would secure the south and west of Ireland 'for the Republic'. The Irish Civil War had begun.

# CHAPTER 3

# THE REPUBLIC OF CORK

Following the outbreak of hostilities at the end of June, the city of Cork found itself cut off from much of Ireland and under IRA military rule. The six-week life of this 'Cork Republic' provides an important context for the popular reaction to the National Army landings in August 1922.

## COMMANDEERING

Immediately after the Free State Army attacked the Four Courts, the Cork City IRA formed two large flying columns totalling about 100 men, and moved on Limerick.[1] Before departing, Republicans equipped themselves in a frenzy of commandeering. They visited clothing shops to seize trench coats, leggings and boots for flying-column fighters. For transportation, they confiscated numerous commercial delivery vehicles, the absence of which wreaked havoc on the local economy.[2] Quartermaster returns from the nearby Cobh Company indicate the cost of such seizures. During the first few weeks of the Civil War, that unit confiscated just over £300 worth of merchandise from local shops – mainly food, clothing, cigarettes and car parts. The adjoining Cork No. 4 Brigade quartermaster requested 100 caps, 300 overcoats and 2,000 pairs of socks.[3] Similar totals would be expected throughout the county.

Taking advantage of the confusion, unaffiliated opportunists wholeheartedly joined in the commandeering.[4] Freebooters began to appear in Cork's Republican courts, most commonly charged with 'demanding drink in the name of the IRA'.[5] One IRA Volunteer apparently acted as his own independent brigade, seizing boots and breeches from five separate shops and paying for them with scribbled receipts from mythical IRA headquarters. He was convicted of robbery later in the month.[6] Lord Mayor Donal Óg O'Callaghan recognised that these seizures, both authorised and unauthorised, created 'a sense of want of security and protection', and promised action.[7]

Civic leaders sought accommodation with Republican authorities. Harbour Commissioner Frank Daly visited Liam Lynch, and was informed that business would be allowed to function as normally as conditions permitted.[8] Labour leaders similarly huddled with the IRA to discuss the war's impact on employment. Cork merchants agreed to keep their doors open and to share the costs of commandeering among themselves. There was additional concern about possible famine if the National Army besieged the city.[9] Responding to 'scaremongers', Donal Óg O'Callaghan formed the Cork Food Committee to protect local supplies. During the Republican occupation of Cork, the food committee ensured the continuation of the city's commercial life.[10]

## REPUBLICAN GOVERNANCE

The Republicans introduced strong measures to end irregular confiscations and looting attributed to the IRA. The Cork No. 1 Brigade announced that all of its commandeering would now be conducted via requisition forms signed by the brigade quartermaster, Seán MacSwiney.[11] Merchants should consider anyone seizing goods without a requisition to be 'common thieves'. The IRA promised to honour the requisitions at their headquarters, emphasising that 'the credit of this brigade has always been good and we mean to keep it so'. The same day, the 1st Southern

Division ordered all motor vehicles to carry a driving permit stamped by the local IRA brigade, and these were checked at road blocks around Cork. This seems to have been undertaken both for internal security and to prevent the continuing unauthorised seizures of vehicles.[12]

In a further move to regain order, Republican police ordered public houses to close promptly at 10 p.m., and threatened to shut any establishment serving alcoholic drinks to intoxicated patrons.[13] A Republican publicity department took charge of censoring the *Cork Examiner* and *Cork Constitution* newspapers, initially to protect sensitive military matters. Under the direction of Erskine Childers (working at the Victoria Hotel), the *Examiner* evolved into an IRA mouthpiece distributed throughout Republican-controlled Munster. The Republicans used it to offset the overwhelmingly hostile national press, which echoed government propaganda and operated under Free State censorship. At least one prominent pro-Treaty politician believed the *Examiner* was moving local opinion towards the Republicans.[14]

Anti-Treaty Cumann na mBan members added to the effort by painting slogans and hanging propaganda posters on walls around the city. They carried messages such as 'Soldiers of the Republic Are True to that Oath';[15] 'Into the Empire, Over Cathal Brugha's Dead Body'; 'Scrap the Treaty and Stop the War'; and 'Collins is Marching on Cork – Why Not Belfast?'[16] Writer and IRA Volunteer Seán O'Fáolain also produced a small sheet called *The Republican War News*, under the anti-Treaty flag.[17]

ISOLATION

Within the first week of the Civil War, Cork was isolated from Dublin and Free State-controlled Ireland. Intermittent telegraph and telephone communications were finally severed with Dublin, but not with London. Newspapers carried racing results from

England, but no mention of fighting in the midlands. Railway, road and boat transportation between Dublin and 'the real capital' was also cut.

The break in communications presented special problems to William Egan & Sons, silversmiths, run by pro-Treaty Deputy Mayor Barry Egan.[18] All silver pieces are stamped with a special hallmark to denote the maker. Egan's hallmark was the city of Cork's coat of arms: a ship between two towers. By law, assayers in Dublin had to inspect the pieces for silver quality; those passing muster were stamped with a harp. However, conditions in July 1922 prevented Egan's pieces from being assayed in Dublin. Egan continued to produce pieces for export, and decided to make a special hallmark to denote that they had not been assayed. At the suggestion of writer Oliver St John Gogarty, Egan slightly altered the Cork coat of arms, removing one of the three masts in the ship between the towers. This special hallmark was only used for sixty-five pieces produced during the Republican occupation of Cork, and was then destroyed. These 'Republican Silver' pieces are now highly valuable collector's items.

Egan was able to export his silver pieces because the Port of Cork remained open to shipping. Foreign correspondents entered and left the city with impunity, utilising the boat service to Liverpool and Holyhead. Republicans had little choice but to keep the port open or risk destroying the city's economy. The Provisional Government similarly refrained from blockading Cork for the same reason, though theirs was an easier decision since the Royal Navy ensured that no military supplies reached Republican Cork. Historian John Linge reports that up to July 1922, the British intercepted and inspected seventy-six ships off the Irish coast.[19] Some of these searches caused alarm in Cork, including an episode in June when the cruiser HMS *Danze* fired across the bow of a German steamer incorrectly suspected of running arms.[20]

Throughout these weeks, powerful British warships prowled Cork Harbour. Though port traffic suffered, a limited amount of freight continued to arrive from non-Irish ports. The Republicans soon eyed the harbour income held within the city's granite landmark, the Cork Customs House.

## RAISING REVENUE

Cork merchants paid duty on goods flowing through the Port of Cork. These taxes were held in the Customs House under the eye of the collector of customs, now employed by the Provisional Government. The Republicans decided to redirect this revenue, rather than allow it to boost the pro-Treaty government's war chest. At the beginning of July, the Cork No. 1 Brigade's 'department of civil administration' occupied the Customs House and placed its collection office under IRA control.[21] The revenue was still collected by customs officials and lodged in the government's account at the Bank of Ireland. However, it was then transferred into an IRA account opened at the same bank.[22] Merchants continued to pay the duties 'without murmur or protest', since they had technically complied with the tax laws: whatever happened to the government's duties after the merchants had paid them was not their concern.

The operation generated large sums for the IRA, bringing in £2,000 per day, £12,000 per week, a total of £45,000 by 17 July, and nearly £100,000 by the time the Republicans abandoned the city.[23] This was part of a concerted effort by Munster Republicans to fund their operations by seizing Free State tax revenue.[24] Similar collections were made in Waterford, Killarney and Tralee, under an IRA 1st Southern Division civil administration department headed by former civil servant Andrew O'Sullivan.

Republicans now bought goods with cheques from the Cork No. 1 Brigade's bank account. The scheme satisfied both shopkeepers and Republicans: merchants no longer shouldered the cost of IRA requisitions and there was reduced resentment about the IRA's seizure of goods. Problems did emerge, however, following the IRA's evacuation of Cork in August, when the Bank of Ireland froze the brigade's account and refused to honour outstanding cheques. The brigade quartermaster, Seán MacSwiney, advised shopkeepers to apply for government compensation and to claim that the goods were requisitioned under duress. As far as IRA cheques paid to shops were concerned, he suggested tactfully that 'it might be as well for the applicant not to mention this'.[25]

Demonstrating more fiscal ingenuity, the IRA's civil administration department also targeted local income tax. Because of the disturbed conditions and a boycott of the British administration in 1920–1, many citizens and businesses did not pay their local rates and income taxes. Cork Corporation, for example, reported that only 50 per cent of its local rates had been collected in the last six months of 1921. According to IRA calculations, city residents owed a remarkable £1,250,000 in uncollected tax revenue, and the Republicans believed they could recover a third of that total.[26]

In mid-July, the Republicans occupied the Inland Revenue office on the South Mall. To foil their plans, District Tax Inspector Charles White 'hopped it to England', but was arrested at Cappoquin trying to cross IRA lines. This pillar of Cork society was returned to Cork under escort and ordered to report daily to IRA headquarters. During his absence, the tax staff worked 'as usual', under the watchful eyes of two former revenue clerks now serving with the Republicans.[27] The surveyor of taxes similarly bolted for England, leaving his assessment copies with Frank Daly (pro-Treaty chairman of the Cork Harbour Board), who hid them in flour bags in Sutton's coal and outfitter's warehouse on the South Mall. However, the originals were not destroyed and the Republicans soon seized them.[28]

Having reviewed the records, the Cork No. 1 Brigade sent staggeringly high bills to the city's largest firms and factories, explaining that they had enjoyed tax-free profits during the previous two years. According to one correspondent, 'This communication came as a bombshell to the taxpayers.'[29] Members of the Chamber of Commerce and Cork Employers' Federation gathered to discuss the situation, and asked solicitor Maurice Healy for legal advice. The former All-For-Ireland MP told them that it was both inadvisable and unethical to pay the IRA tax charge. A request also came from Michael Collins, via his sister Mary Collins-Powell, that businesses refrain from paying.[30] Emboldened, the merchants informed the IRA that they would shut their doors and discharge their staff rather than comply, which forced the Republicans' hand. Blaming Healy for this truculence, an IRA squad visited his office, escorted him home, watched him pack a bag and then placed him aboard the evening boat to Holyhead.

After examining the revenue books, the Republicans sent additional bills to the Cork Corporation and Harbour Board, asking for refunds of income taxes paid to those bodies. The detailed bill (£1,470 to the Corporation and £4,530 to the Harbour Board) shows an effort by the Republicans to present their actions as legal and proper. These exact figures were later charged by the Free State revenue commissioners.[31] Around the same time, the IRA faced defiance at Ford's tractor factory, the city's largest employer. IRA engineers attempted to commandeer pig iron for the construction of mines and grenades. However, the American factory manager, Edward Grace, told the Republicans that if they seized anything, he would shut the factory and throw 2,000 staff out of work. He also refused to allow the premises or his workers to be used to construct an IRA armoured car. Grace in fact had no intention of closing the plant, but on 2 August he asked his employers in Flint, Michigan, USA, to 'send me in plain English via commercial a strong cablegram ordering me to close plant entirely if any troops interfere too much'. With enough trouble on their hands already, the Republicans did not call Grace's bluff.[32]

## THE WAR'S REAL CAPITAL

The Republicans exercised little outward coercion during their time in power. IRA Volunteers occupied few buildings beyond Cork Men's Gaol, the Customs House, Union Quay RIC barracks and Victoria military barracks. Though there was no crackdown on pro-Treaty internal dissidents, the Republicans did check for Free State infiltrators at roadblocks on thoroughfares entering and leaving Cork, and boat passengers were also questioned and searched. In late July, Free State Army spy Murt O'Connell was arrested by the Republicans when trying to leave the city by boat. His capture seems to have triggered a raid on the pro-Treaty political party rooms at 74 Grand Parade and the arrest of pro-Treaty election agents Joe McCarthy and Michael Mehigan. The latter had been working covertly with the Provisional Government to send Cork recruits to the Free State Army.[33] However, the City IRA's vaunted intelligence service, stripped of its officers during the hostilities, critically failed to uncover a much more ambitious effort to mobilise Cork ex-soldiers for the Free State. Republican control of the rebel capital was visible, yet shallow, as events would prove.

As the 'line-fighting' continued for weeks in Limerick, Tipperary and Waterford, Republicans travelled through the city on their way to and from the front. A visiting newspaper correspondent described them as, 'tired, weary-looking, war-worn, covered with whitish mud'.[34] He wrote of lorries passing with armed men singing 'A Soldier's Song', while Liam de Róiste noted that these Republicans wore their caps backwards to denote active service. The correspondent was more impressed by the fifty-man IRA cavalry unit passing through the city, travelling to its base in nearby Ballincollig. Every Cork IRA battalion provided one mounted Volunteer for the cavalry force; units were advised to commandeer the best hunting horses in their area, as their jumping abilities could be useful. One such mount was reportedly a famous point-to-point racer, and the Republicans declined a £300 offer for his return.[35] In mid-July, the anti-Treaty Cumann na mBan opened a receiving depot for IRA Volunteers passing through the city, to provide meals and rest.[36] This was modelled on canteens operated during the First World War by Cork Unionists, to assist British troops in transit.

Free State prisoners of war (POWs) caused excitement when they arrived in the city. By the end of July, the Republicans were holding 200 prisoners at the Victoria barracks stockade and the Cork Men's Gaol.[37] Over forty of them came from Cork city (mainly from the pro-Treaty C Company, 1st Battalion, IRA), captured near Kilmallock. Local women applauded the prisoners as they were marched through the streets, and families frequently gathered outside the gates of the gaol to shout messages to loved ones. Overwhelmed by visitor requests, the Republicans tried to transfer these prisoners out of Cork, as 'We're damned from people calling here the whole day.'[38] IRA attempts to secure a chaplain for the prisoners proved no more successful, yielding only insults from the Catholic Church. Bishop Cohalan ordered his priests to refuse to attend the POWs, 'giving as his reason that the authority of the bishops had been repudiated'.[39] Cohalan told a Republican commander, 'he did not recognise our authority nor would he ever be prepared to do so', and refused to speak to him further.[40] IRA Volunteer Seán Hendrick recalled being denounced at mass by a priest, who 'spoke about looters, robbers and bank-robbers', before promising of the Republicans, 'they'll rob ye, leave ye without any money'.[41] Bishop Cohalan and his clergy were notably absent from consultations with the IRA or involvement in peace efforts. A few weeks after the Republicans abandoned Cork, Cohalan essentially excommunicated IRA Volunteers, and ordered his diocese to support the new state.[42]

BESIEGED

The Civil War made no intrusion on many aspects of social life in Cork. Train services continued in Republican-held areas of the county. During the long weeks of summer, athletics meetings attracted city residents to nearby towns. GAA fixtures proceeded normally, as did the harrier meets and horse races. The Cork regatta was a success, with dozens of rowers racing up the river. The August Bank Holiday drew enormous crowds to nearby coastal resorts on special trains. Concerts, public talks and theatre programmes went on largely uninterrupted. There was much excitement when a 25-foot basking shark washed up close to the city, having been skewered dramatically on the bow of the mail packet SS *Classic* off Ballycotton. Hundreds gathered every day at Tivoli to view the corpse. However, despite such public amusements, an undercurrent of dread flowed beneath the surface of Cork.[43]

The city suffered from the strain of isolation and pending combat, especially as the war entered its third and fourth weeks.[44] The economy, already in recession, slipped into a depression. One correspondent reported, 'business is at a standstill', while to another, 'enterprise is dead'.[45] Some of the large provisions and drapery shops shut their doors for want of stock. Fearing Republican commandeering, their non-Cork suppliers would not risk importing goods into the city, and businesses could not communicate with Irish buyers and suppliers because of severed telegraph and mail services. The lack of shipping resulted in the discharge of quay labourers, while railway workers on numerous lines faced dismissal. The Port of Cork suffered £1,700 a week losses in shipping revenue. In mid-July, the Lee Boot Factory closed, while the *Cork Constitution* shut its doors rather than submit to IRA censorship. At the end of July, the Provisional Government stopped paying for local government services. Construction projects were postponed for fear of destruction in the anticipated street fighting in Cork, and fuel supply shortages threatened to shut the Ford factory. The Munster & Leinster Bank could not produce balance sheets for its annual meeting, supplies of silver dried up because of hoarding and banks withdrew cashier cheques and currency from circulation. Postage stamps also ran out, causing Republicans to issue their own. (As in the case of 'Republican Silver', these Cork Republic stamps later became collector's items.)[46]

The Republicans struggled to keep the economy functioning amid the turmoil. The IRA ordered closed shops to reopen their doors. Republican Lord Mayor O'Callaghan announced that after nearly two years of delays, the Corporation would begin the reconstruction of Patrick's Street, providing precious jobs for the building sector. The Great Southern and Western Railway threatened to discharge all rail workers if train services were disrupted, but IRA officers prohibited the district superintendent and other railway officials from locking out their staff, rather than allow 'an atmosphere against us'.[47] Yet, despite such actions, the Cork economy continued to decline.

To labour leaders, the situation was untenable. Unemployment was approaching 8,000 – over 30 per cent of the male working population.[48] The ITGWU reported 1,800 idle members in Cork, with many homeless who were sleeping on the quayside or in the Mardyke bandstand.[49] 'The state they now found themselves in was becoming desperate,' argued union leader Tim Kenneally, 'for bakers were refusing bread, milkmen milk, and landlords were giving notices to quit for non-payment of rent.'[50] 'The key to the situation is work,' reported a Free State Army intelligence officer.

'A man, on seeing some lorries with armed men pass by, said to his companion: "If they were as hungry as we are, they would not have much stomach for fight".'[51] 'People live from hand to mouth, from day to day,' wrote one correspondent, 'not knowing what the morrow may bring.'[52] The Cork Trades Council demanded something be done to stop 'the cry of hungry children and starving workers'; the council president complained, 'thousands and thousands are starving in the city, and who cares?'[53]

Local residents also feared the destruction of Cork in the coming fighting, having read about destructive fires and shelling in Dublin, Limerick and Waterford. Savvy insurance agents advertised policies that covered property damage in civil war and riots.[54] Newspapers beyond Cork reported that thousands had been killed in the city, and other dramatic headlines promised a 'last stand in Cork', 'the end is drawing nigh', 'Cork's day of trial', 'The curse of Cain – economic ruin ahead of Cork City'.[55] The Cork Lunatic Asylum reported a surge in new admissions, which the medial superintendent attributed to 'the political atmosphere and unrest'.[56]

## PEACE MOVEMENT

In the tense atmosphere, a peace movement arose from Cork labour and commercial leaders. In mid-July, an ITGWU delegation appeared at the Cork Harbour Board to appeal for employment for its idle members. 'The unemployed had shown great patience,' remarked a union leader, 'but the time had come when they could stick it no longer.' Pro-Treaty leader Liam de Róiste questioned the continuation of combat. 'It is time for the unarmed people to ask the authorities on both sides what it is all about,' he said, 'I myself fail to see what it is about.' The Harbour Board then adopted a motion calling for an immediate armistice and a peace conference. Over the next few days, commercial, labour and civic bodies adopted the Harbour Board's peace proposal, which led to a special conference at the Cork Customs House.[57]

Representatives of virtually every civic group in Cork attended the peace meeting. Speaker after speaker appealed for national unity and denounced a conflict that brought only 'devastation, destruction and desolation'. The meeting formed the People's Rights Association and called for a settlement based on the following four points:

1   Civil war is avoidable.
2   'Immediate cessation of hostilities'.
3   Assemble the Third Dáil immediately to act as the country's only recognised authority.
4   If the Free State government and IRA Executive fail to reach a peace agreement, the Third Dáil will order both sides to honour a ceasefire.[58]

A second meeting attracted twelve TDs, mainly from Cork and Kerry, including IRA leaders Seán Moylan and Seán MacSwiney, and pro-Treaty IRA officer Seán Hales. Once again, speakers appealed for the IRA to come under government control, ruled by a unified Army Council. The Provisional Government was also subjected to heavy criticism for launching the war before it opened the new (Third) Dáil, and refusing to convene the parliament, 'in direct contravention of the fundamental rights of the people'. The association sent a delegation to Dublin to ask the speaker of the Dáil to summon that assembly; if he did not, they would call for all TDs to gather in Cork.[59] A 'Women's Peace Meeting' was also held at the Cork courthouse, where its organiser proclaimed to a boisterous crowd, 'no individual despot should assume the right to proclaim war'. Similar peace meetings in Tralee and Skibbereen also called for a national ceasefire.[60]

For the Provisional Government, these peace moves were unwelcome. Though pro-Treaty TDs had been elected to form a coalition government with anti-Treaty Republicans, they had scrapped that agreement and launched the Civil War without the sanction of the Dáil. Provisional Government leaders continued to delay calling parliament into session until after they had won a clear military victory over the Republicans. Otherwise, the new Dáil might prevent the disarming and dismantling of the IRA, which the pro-Treaty party considered to be essential to long-term political stability. A ceasefire would only strengthen the IRA at the moment of its demise.

Responding to Cork peace feelers, IRA chief of staff Liam Lynch offered a truce and IRA allegiance to the Dáil, if the latter acted in the name of the 'Government of the Republic' rather than the Irish Free State. However, his counterpart Michael Collins demanded the Republicans' unconditional surrender. Collins further condemned the People's Rights Association for address-ing Lynch as 'General' and using the term 'Civil War' rather than his preferred phrase of 'police action'.[61] The speaker of the Dáil, Eoin MacNeill, similarly rebuffed the Cork peace delegation and refused to call the Dáil into session.

Evidence indicates that a strong majority of the Cork popu-lation opposed the Republicans' waging of Civil War. But the People's Rights Association also showed that most residents would have preferred a peaceful resolution to the conflict. Much support for the Treaty was based on an end to all fighting, rather than continued bloodshed confined to Irish combatants. The Irish Labour Party strongly endorsed the peace movement under a Civil War mantra of 'a plague on both your houses'. To the *Voice of Labour*, the Cork IRA had filled Ireland with 'pride and courage' in the fight against England and therefore deserved an honourable settlement:

These men have a right to consideration. They have a right to respect. They are not brigands or looters, or riff raff. They were deceived by the Dáil cabinet, by Dáil Éireann, and by all the complexity which has gone on since December last. They have a right to be saved for the nation and not eliminated, if it can be done. And rest assured, bellicose pen wielders, that if you get your way, and this war is fought to a finish, it is not going to be so easy as it may look from Dublin. We say: Stop it now.[62]

In Cork, the ITGWU's new 'Unemployed Central Committee' prepared to launch a general strike to stop the fighting. One leader promised, 'the unemployed, were indifferent to the government of the country whether they be Republicans or Free Staters, but a settlement must come'.[63] The Cork Ex-Soldiers' Federation promised to join any such work stoppage. On Bank Holiday Monday, 8 August, posters appeared around the city announcing a mass meeting of the unemployed for the following Sunday. But events overtook the Cork Labour Party. That same Bank Holiday, National Army troops sailed into Cork Harbour. The battle for Cork had begun.

# CHAPTER 4

# DEFENDING CORK

A popular misconception of the Irish Civil War is that the Republicans never expected Free State Army coastal landings behind their lines. In fact, IRA officers feared sea landings, and took steps to prevent them. However, Republican Munster did not have sufficient resources to forestall an amphibious assault.

## CORK NO. 1 BRIGADE POSITION

On the first day of the Dublin fighting, Cork No. 1 Brigade officers assembled at Union Quay barracks to decide their plans.[1] Brigade commander Seán O'Hegarty spoke forcefully against entering the Civil War, arguing that 'the whole country would be destroyed, the people would be against us'.[2] O'Hegarty was a decade older than most of the officers, ruled his brigade with an iron fist and had dominated Cork's physical-force Republicanism for over twenty years. Despite this high standing, O'Hegarty was outvoted thirteen votes to three; one prominent IRA leader found it, 'amazing in 1922 that the fellows stood out against Seán Hegarty [*sic*]'.[3] Taking a neutral stance, O'Hegarty and his brigade adjutant, Dominic Sullivan, resigned from the IRA on the spot, as did the commanders of the 5th Battalion and 9th Battalion (the latter included Passage West, hereafter called Passage). O'Hegarty was replaced by his vice-commander, Mick Leahy of Cobh, 'a good fighting man' and a trained marine engineer.[4] Leahy was best known for his skilled capture of the Carrigtwohill RIC barracks in January 1920, the first British post taken since the Easter Rising.

1st Southern Division adjutant and intelligence officer Florrie O'Donoghue also resigned rather than become involved in the war. O'Donoghue was a great loss to Republican military intelligence, where he rivalled Michael Collins for effectiveness. He was replaced by his Cork subordinate, Seán Culhane, a dapper draper's assistant who had previously acted as an operative rather than an administrator. 'He has a face like a cherub,' one harsh colleague said of Culhane, 'and he's in charge of intelligence and he hasn't got any.'[5] As will be shown, the Cork IRA's failure to prevent the Passage landing can in many ways be attributed to poor intelligence. Had O'Donoghue remained on the scene, such failings might have been avoided. His neutral stance also reflected wider ambivalence within the Cork No. 1 Brigade towards the war. Hundreds of previously committed Republicans subsequently abstained from fighting their fellow Irishmen. In late 1922, O'Donoghue and O'Hegarty formed the 'Neutral IRA' organisation, which attracted thousands of members from the various Cork brigades.

Despite the success of the *Upnor* raid, at the outset of the war Cork Republicans faced a massive deficit in war supplies. While pro-Treaty forces were armed, equipped and effectively paid by the British Empire, the IRA depended on the citizenry for their upkeep. For example, by early July 1922, the British government had handed over 355 vehicles to the Provisional Government, including 81 with armoured plating.[6] The Cork Republicans, however, had to seize vehicles, petrol and spare parts from the local population. To construct two armoured cars, the Republicans went searching house to house for scrap metal for plating, which they painstakingly fashioned themselves.[7] The government paid Free State soldiers, which enticed many to join in the severe economic recession. IRA Volunteers served without payment and were in danger of losing precious jobs while on active service. Brigade commander Michael Leahy complained: 'Our good men had jobs, and they had only the wasters and idlers to provide the garrisons for barracks.'[8] While a part-time army worked well in a guerrilla situation, it was disastrous in a conventional campaign such as the first stage of the Irish Civil War.

## WAR STRATEGY

After the surrender of the Four Courts, IRA chief of staff Liam Lynch directed operations from his Mallow headquarters. Despite his deficiencies as a military leader, Lynch grasped the implications of conflict with the Provisional Government. He initially intended to clear western and southern Ireland of Free State forces, while IRA guerrilla units severed his opponents' transportation, supply and communication lines. With Dublin fully isolated, Lynch believed the Provisional Government would capitulate in a few days.[9]

At the outset of the war, Munster Republicans formed their most experienced fighters into columns and sent them to Limerick. In this first week, the IRA cleared Counties Cork and Kerry of National Army troops. Other IRA units, including the Cork City column, pushed into Limerick city. Along the way, they captured or forced the evacuation of numerous Free State garrisons, taking scores of prisoners. The Republicans intended to first clear Limerick city of National Army troops, then move against isolated Free State garrisons in Clare and Galway, before linking up with Republican concentrations in Sligo and Mayo. They would then march on Dublin. However, this plan unravelled almost at the start, foiled by the Republican defeat in Limerick city.

As Pádraig Óg Ó Ruairc has shown in his book, *The Battle for Limerick city*, Lynch made a disastrous error by signing a truce with National Army generals Michael Brennan and Donal O'Hannigan in Limerick city. Lynch gambled on pulling off a 'glorious' coup, in which Brennan and O'Hannigan's troops would take a neutral stance in the hostilities. With these National Army soldiers out of the way, the Republicans could quickly clear the rest of Munster and Connaught, and then focus on Leinster. Lynch could probably have achieved the same result had he simply thrown his superior force immediately against the weak Free State garrison in Limerick city. As it turned out, Brennan and O'Hannigan had played for time, exploiting Lynch's desire to avoid bloodshed. Having built up their forces, they broke the ceasefire without notice. Following an intense nine-day battle, National Army troops finally drove the Republicans from Limerick.[10]

The Limerick truce damaged the morale of the IRA fighters, who questioned its wisdom. About 100 Cork city Republicans had engaged in the street fighting and they fell back in good order but were demoralised. One veteran recalled, 'they were very depressed at retreating', while another believed the defeat 'is what finished our fellows'.[11]

Having lost Limerick city, Liam Lynch adjusted his strategy. His Munster forces still held a line running from Waterford to Limerick, but faced mounting attacks from the Free State Army. Lynch intended to absorb these blows, and to suck more National Army troops into Munster.[12] Operating behind the Free State front, IRA flying columns (well supplied with automatic weapons and mines) could then sever the government supply lines. If the Republicans failed to hold their Munster line, they would simply resume guerrilla warfare. Guerrilla fighting was what they did best, and Lynch believed the IRA would beat the Free State in a war of attrition, just as it had (in his mind) defeated the British army.

This was a logical strategy, but it contained a series of misjudgements:

1   The plan failed to end the war quickly. Financed and supplied by the British government, the Free State Army grew stronger every day that the conflict continued.
2   It committed the IRA to fighting both conventionally and unconventionally. Built as a guerrilla army, the IRA had to either reorganise as a conventional force, or revert to guerrilla tactics. By doing neither, it suffered the worst of both worlds, which led to a string of defeats.
3   Lynch underestimated how much these defeats would demoralise the IRA Volunteers and damage public support.
4   Lynch did not recognise that the IRA could not resume guerrilla war without popular support; and his strategy did nothing to swing public opinion towards the Republicans.
5   Finally, Lynch failed to address the primary reason for public opposition to the IRA: if the Republicans overthrew the Free State government, they faced a second prolonged guerrilla war with Britain. The public had made it clear that dominion status was preferable to war with a global superpower.

Despite Lynch's strategic shortcomings, few alternatives were offered by Cork city Republicans. One column of city men joined the Cork No. 1 Brigade contingent in Limerick, and engaged in 'line fighting' around Kilmallock over the next three weeks. A second body of up to 100 Cork City IRA Volunteers anchored the Republican defence of Waterford, under the command of Mick Murphy and Pa Murray.[13] All told, between 150 and 250 Republicans were probably out of the city in this period. They were the most experienced IRA Volunteers in Cork, thus the city organisation was stripped of its leadership. This was a continuation of the

War of Independence practice that gathered top Republicans into flying columns, to be supported by the rest of the IRA organisation. Using the Republican elite as shock troops made sense when the IRA tried hurriedly to capture Limerick. However, as the weeks went by, this fighting force was ground down without any replacements being prepared by the IRA.

Unlike the National Army, the IRA in Cork did not build a larger, full-time military force, leavened with its best officers. Instead, the Republican elite was concentrated in a few columns utilised as fighters rather than leaders. For example, brigade transport officer Jim Grey drove an armoured car, rather than managing vehicle transport for the whole brigade. During the Limerick fighting, one of his gunners was the brigade intelligence officer, Seán Culhane; and Dan Healy, of the brigade intelligence staff, drove another armoured car.[14] Instead of instructing replacement troops, brigade training officer Seán Murray led a platoon-sized column in Limerick. Pa Murray commanded a similar column in Waterford, though he had initially been placed in charge of harbour defence. The Republicans responded to immediate needs instead of anticipating future developments. The overall strength of their organisation weakened just as the tempo of the war increased. When placed under severe strain by the National Army's landing at Passage, the Cork IRA collapsed.

## PROTECTING THE COAST

IRA leaders did not forget the vulnerable coastline behind them. GHQ director of operations Seán Moylan warned in mid-July of seaborne landings. Tom Hales, OC Cork No. 3 Brigade, thought the Free State troops would land in Kinsale; Mick Leahy, OC Cork No. 1 Brigade, believed they would target Youghal and Ballycotton; Kerry's controversial ex-brigadier, Paddy Cahill, predicted landings in Dingle, Tarbert and Fenit; Pat O'Sullivan, OC of the

8th Battalion, Cork No. 1 Brigade, foresaw an invasion at Union Hall; Sandow O'Donovan, vice-commander of the Cork No. 1 Brigade, successfully identified Passage as a destination. For IRA leaders, envisioning an amphibious assault was not the problem – the issue was determining where and when it would occur.[15] Prior notice of the invasion would have to come from Republicans in Dublin, where seaborne National Army troops would embark.

The IRA's Dublin Brigade was not up to the task, as by mid-July it was falling apart. Brigade fighters were spent in successive defeats at the Four Courts, O'Connell Street and Blessington. Though Ernie O'Malley assumed overall command of Republican forces in the capital, the situation continued to deteriorate. The National Army absorbed Michael Collins' IRA intelligence staff, and its members knew Dublin officers by sight as well as the location of safe houses. They decimated the Dublin Brigade's junior and senior leadership, with O'Malley consistently reporting heavy losses among officers and his inability to field an intelligence department.[16] The Dubliners' backs were finally broken on 5 August, in a failed attempt to destroy all the bridges leading into the city following repeated orders from Lynch to sever Free State communications.[17] National Army intelligence caught wind of the operation and swept up the IRA wrecking parties, capturing many of the city's remaining activists.[18] Had the effort been successful, it might have panicked the Provisional Government into pulling troops out of Munster to guard the capital. Instead, the bridge fiasco left the Dublin Brigade effectively dead in the water. Owing to these cumulative setbacks, the Dubliners were incapable of warning Munster Republicans about troops sailing for the south. Without this advance notice, Munster could not concentrate its defenders to contest the landings. In Dublin's defence, IRA GHQ failed to prioritise the gathering of crucial coastal invasion intelligence.

Munster Republicans needed to know precisely where and when the National Army would land, because they had too much coastline to cover. In Cork, Kerry and Waterford, there were at least a dozen potential landing spots. One Cork IRA veteran recalled, 'Our numbers were hardly adequate … and with a wide perimeter, too wide to be adequately held.'[19]

By 9 July, 1st Southern Division engineers had mined piers and approaches to likely landing spots, prepared bridges for destruction, and erected road barricades guarded by riflemen. At the end of July, the IRA denied the Free State Army proper landing piers. Cork No. 1 Brigade blew up Youghal Quay as well as Ballycotton Pier, the site of the spectacular *Upnor* raid just a few months earlier. Kerry Republicans were ordered to wreck Tarbert Pier, while the West Cork IRA destroyed the dock at Union Hall. When another IRA party prepared to blow Castletownbere Pier, they were physically attacked by the misnamed Father Lamb, who had earlier broken the rifle of a Republican sentry: 'He grappled with one of these men, and after about ten minutes wrestling he withdrew,' reported Commandant Gibbs Ross sardonically, 'our man being the victor this time.'[20] The Republicans took the sea threat seriously, manning coastguard stations, posting coastal sentries and garrisoning likely landing points. Yet the IRA did not have enough troops both to hold the Limerick/Waterford line and prevent an amphibious assault. When the invasion came, Republican coastal defences proved to be far too flimsy.

## PREVENTING A LANDING IN CORK HARBOUR

As the de facto rebel capital, Cork city was the most obvious target for a sea invasion. Cork Harbour is one of the world's great deepwater ports, formed from a large estuary at the mouth of the River Lee. The city is located roughly eleven miles upstream, in the north-west corner of the harbour. Built in the river valley, Cork city is shaped like a bowl, with steep hills on each side overlooking the flat land of the city centre. Two channels of the River Lee run through the city, criss-crossed by numerous bridges. The river flows on into the inland bay of Lough Mahon, whose shore skirts the city's eastern suburbs of Blackrock, Douglas and Rochestown. This entire area is known as Upper Harbour. From Lough Mahon, a narrow river channel runs past Passage and empties into the much larger bay, called Lower Harbour. Small shore communities dot Lower Harbour, including Crosshaven, Monkstown, Ringaskiddy, Whitegate, Aghada and Cobh. The main port town of Cobh sits on Great Island, connected to the mainland by bridges at the end of a narrow peninsula. Lower Harbour also includes two large islands that were still being used as British military bases in 1922: Spike Island and Haulbowline. The British retained two other forts at the harbour gate: Forts Camden and Carlisle. The overall area very roughly resembles an hourglass, with Upper and Lower Harbours representing the two bulb chambers, joined at the middle by the narrow channel at Passage.

Cork Harbour offered an invading army multiple landing places. In Lower Harbour, Free State troops could dock unopposed at any of the three British Treaty forts (Camden, Carlisle or Spike Island) or the Haulbowline naval shipyard, and use them to stage a later advance. In July, Michael Collins asked the British cabinet to hand over one of the forts for just such a venture, but his appeal was rejected. (Sensitive to appearances of Irish sovereignty, Collins refused to access the forts while they were occupied by the British.)[21] Cobh offered another target, attractive because of its docking facilities and location that allowed troops to bypass Cork. Its chief drawback, however, was its connection to the mainland by two bridges that could easily be destroyed, exposing soldiers to dangerous bottlenecks. Crosshaven was a different option, but it lay a dozen miles from Cork by poor roads. Passage provided an alternative, but it was situated on a narrow river channel that could yield dangerous crossfire; it was also seven miles from Cork, with access by a single road. A mile or two downriver, Ringaskiddy and Monkstown offered more choices, but they were connected to Cork by the same river road that ran through Passage. And entry via Passage, Ringaskiddy or Monkstown still placed the invaders south of Cork city and the River Lee. To cross the river, troops would need to fight their way through the city centre and seize bridgeheads across both river channels. The simplest but most audacious plan was to steam all the way upriver, land in the city itself and capture the critical bridges intact before the Republicans could respond. Ultimately, General Emmet Dalton chose the latter option.

When contemplating the defence of Cork, IRA leaders saw themselves as facing both the National Army and the Royal Navy. The Republicans assumed that the British would actively support Free State operations in Cork, which indeed became formal Admiralty policy at the end of August.[22] Despite the British evacuation of Cobh, numerous Royal Navy warships still patrolled Lower Harbour. Even the smallest seagoing vessel could blast the IRA from any defensive position. In late July an IRA coastguard garrison experienced a demonstration of British naval firepower at Lackeen, near Kenmare, County Kerry. After IRA Volunteers fired on a British shore party, the unfortunately named mine-sweeper HMS *Badminton* destroyed the station with shellfire. IRA defenders simply could not protect themselves from British naval guns. As a result, the Cork No. 1 Brigade made little effort to defend Lower Harbour, since it was essentially already in British and, therefore, also in Free State hands.

## REPUBLICAN DREADNOUGHTS, THE PASSAGE GARRISON AND CITY DEFENCES

The Cork No. 1 Brigade commander, Mick Leahy, was a Cobh native, a former shipyard worker and a trained maritime engineer with seagoing experience. He approached the harbour defence in a practical way and with reasonable foresight. Armed with only small arms and some rifle grenades, Leahy's forces could not prevent vessels from entering Lower Harbour or docking in Cobh. As a result, Leahy concentrated on confining invading troops to Cobh and its Great Island; preventing hostile vessels from navigating upriver to Cork; and stationing a force at Passage to both contest a landing there and control the main Cork road. He also occupied Roche's Point lighthouse to monitor shipping, and secured numerous small craft to enable local garrisons to inspect approaching vessels.

According to Royal Navy reports, Republicans were 'apprehensive of a landing of Free State troops on Great Island'.[23] In response, the Cobh IRA moved its base from the Belmont huts (formerly Royal Navy property) in Cobh to Fota House on Fota Island, adjoining Great Island. There Republicans trenched the road and constructed defensive positions, at one point compelling Cobh dockworkers to assist, which did not improve their local popularity. On the Cobh side of Belvelly Bridge (a road bridge), the IRA dug trenches and built barricades facing Cobh, to prevent hostile troops from crossing to the mainland. Cork No. 1 Brigade provided fifteen mines with which to destroy the Fota railway bridge (thus severing the Cork/Cobh railway link) and Belvelly Bridge. The Cobh IRA also mounted Lewis guns atop three cars, to act as patrol vehicles along the shoreline road. Any National troops landing in Cobh (most probably at Rushbrooke shipyard) would now face considerable difficulty in getting off Great Island.[24]

Ships steaming upriver to Cork city had to navigate a tight channel that constricts to some 100 metres wide in certain spots. At the narrowest part of the channel (on Lough Mahon, about halfway between Passage and the Cork Customs House) the Republicans moored the 'IRA navy'. The fleet was composed of two dredging barges, the *No. 1 Hopper* and the *Owenabuee*, operated by the Cork Harbour Board to clear mud from the channel. In early July, the IRA commandeered these 'Republican dreadnoughts' (as they were called by locals) and their crews, and stationed riflemen and a machine-gun team aboard. Mines were placed in the bilge of each barge, so they could quickly be scuttled to block the channel. Small power boats operating from Black-rock Castle supplied the crews with food and replacements. Every ship navigating the channel had to halt at this IRA boom, which was covered by a machine gun aboard the *Owenabuee*. Republican sentries checked the vessel's destination and sometimes went on board to search passengers. Once the Republicans were satisfied, the blocking barges were pulled apart to allow the ship passage through the gap.[25]

The IRA river boom did not always maintain a warlike appearance. One visiting journalist described the 'lonely vigil' aboard a barge by 'two men armed with rifles and clad in trench coats, caps, and leggings', who seemed like a paramilitary version of Cha and Miah.[26] The barge crews (unaffiliated with the IRA) complained to their union about the new duty; they were not concerned about the hazard of guarding the port from invasion, but objected to working seven days a week and only being paid for six. (The crew expressed satisfaction with the meals provided by the IRA, however.) The Harbour Commission subsequently refused to authorise any overtime pay, and blamed the situation on the IRA. This prompted a socialist commissioner to berate the pro-Treaty Harbour Board's lack of 'backbone' at meekly allowing the IRA to use harbour vessels at the Board's expense, yet shifting the extra cost onto its employees.[27]

Though it is unclear whether the Republican dreadnoughts could have stopped a determined effort to force the channel, they ultimately accomplished their mission. Because of a fear of striking scuttled barges, the Free State assault on Cork was diverted to Passage. The bombs aboard the vessels also generated persistent anxiety in both the National Army and the British Admiralty that the IRA had mined the channel, even though sea mines were beyond Republican technical abilities. Some of the belief in IRA river mines seems to have come from the Republicans themselves, who spread such rumours to discourage an attack.[28] Though untested in battle, the IRA navy proved itself to be an effective psychological weapon.

The final IRA defensive preparations focused on Passage and fell within the remit of the 9th Battalion, Cork No. 1 Brigade. The 9th Battalion was formed in May 1920, very late in Cork terms, which reflected its disorganised state. Companies represented the port towns of Passage, Carrigaline, Crosshaven, Kinsale, Rochestown and Monkstown. Eventually the battalion was divided into two subsections, one based in the Kinsale area and another within the western part of Cork Harbour. Passage and four other companies formed the western harbour area. This was one of the Cork No. 1 Brigade's weakest units and had seen little fighting in the Anglo-Irish War. Instead, its Volunteers focused on arms smuggling and weapons manufacturing.[29]

Quartermaster returns from the 9th Battalion show meagre arms holdings, such as one company possessing five shotguns and three revolvers (sharing sixteen rounds of ammunition), or another with an arsenal of two pistols, eleven shotguns and a grenade. By July 1922, one of the region's five companies (Monkstown) had already defected to the Free State and was secretly drilling under an ex-soldier. Much of the battalion remained neutral in the Civil War, with just eighty-three local Republicans willing to fight their countrymen. Over half of them served in the IRA garrison at Passage.

The Republican headquarters in a granary complex of heavy

stone warehouses overlooked the Passage docks. The garrison fielded forty-six men, including ten officers and three sections of riflemen (seven Volunteers to a section). There were also motor-boat drivers, cooks, machine-gun teams and communication runners. As the 9th Battalion possessed no rifles of its own, the Cork No. 1 Brigade seems to have supplied the garrison with eight rifles and a Lewis machine gun, along with numerous mines. Rifles were distributed to whichever section was on duty (every day and night was divided into duty watches), while the machine gun was manned constantly. Because of a lack of rifles, the remaining Republicans were armed with pistols or shotguns, which severely reduced their firepower.[30]

Cork No. 1 Brigade leaders considered the Passage Volunteers to be second-rate fighters.[31] Few of them had seen any combat or even fired a rifle. Their discipline was also called into question in mid-July. One afternoon, the barracks commander, James Hickey, returned from a drinking binge in nearby Monkstown. Clearly drunk, he ordered the Volunteers to vacate the machine gun, positioned on a balcony overlooking the river. Hickey then fired a fifteen-round burst across the river towards pedestrians on the road in Carrigaloe. Having threatened to shoot a subordinate, Hickey was forcibly disarmed by the battalion commander and subsequently suspended from duty.[32] The episode reflected poorly on the garrison's military standards, which would play a critical role during the battle to come in August.

Not trusting their fate to the Passage IRA, Cork Republicans prepared to fight in the city itself.[33] Defensive positions were selected to deny crossings of the south channel of the River Lee. The Beamish and Crawford Brewery was to act as a central garrison. Besides covering South Gate Bridge and Parliament Bridge, the brewery had thick walls and extensive cellars that could withstand machine-gun and artillery fire. Sutton's coal merchants and the

Munster & Leinster Bank on the South Mall were also chosen as formidable structures that covered the three South Channel Bridges near Cork City Hall. Away from the river, the IRA prepared another strongpoint at Grant's department store, which was on the corner of St Patrick's Street and the Grand Parade, the key intersection in the heart of the city. IRA officers inspected further fallback positions beyond the city centre, across the north channel of the Lee.

The Republicans selected machine-gun and sniping posts in houses among the northside neighbourhoods of Patrick's Hill, Summer Hill and Sunday's Well. Placed on steep slopes overlooking the city centre, these would cover the North Channel river bridges. The IRA apparently prepared for the destruction of all the remaining bridges running from the city west to Macroom. Thus, if the Free State Army seized the south side of Cork city, the IRA could still keep them south of the River Lee. By holding a defensible line along the Lee, the IRA would retain a sizeable portion of north and mid-Cork, mountainous country that included their bases in Macroom, Fermoy and Mallow. The city defences were tactically astute, oriented towards the exposed southern coastal flank.

Overall, the IRA took reasonable precautions to prevent a seaborne invasion of Cork. Things would not be easy for the invading Free State Army.

# CHAPTER 5

# PASSAGE LANDING

Though it passed in the midst of a Civil War in Ireland, the 1922 Bank Holiday on 7 August was typical in many ways. Thousands of town and city residents attended race meetings and even more took excursion trains to coastal resorts around Leinster and Munster. The beach weather was fair and mild, and brief rain showers caused little concern. Visitors paraded along seaside promenades or swam in the sea, essentially ignoring the fighting going on around the country. After enjoying their day out, some boarded return trains while others remained for evening dances. The sun did not set until 9.10 p.m., and they enjoyed the lingering twilight. Some of those strolling on the beach probably noticed two cross-channel ferries cruising south off the Irish coast, as if joining the festivities. They were the *Arvonia* and the *Lady Wicklow*, recently commandeered as troop ships for the Free State Army. Those aboard aimed to end the Irish Civil War with a single, bold stroke.

## PREPARATIONS

Historians have largely credited the idea of the Munster sea landings to Emmet Dalton.[1] The concept was fairly obvious to military planners on both sides, yet proved to be dramatically effective as a result of the draining 'line fighting' across Limerick and Cork. As a trial run, a surprise amphibious assault on Westport, County Mayo, by Dublin-based National Army troops achieved complete success on 24 July 1922. More ambitiously, 450 Free State soldiers landed at Fenit, County Kerry, on 2 August and used heavy machine-gun fire to quickly silence the small IRA coastal garrison. The National Army seized Tralee on the same day, despite stubborn Republican resistance. This operation was the first blow in a powerful Free State punch combination intended to win the war in Munster.[2] The Kerry invasion force was commanded by a member of Michael Collins' inner circle, and included gunmen from Collins' own 'Squad', and a military intelligence component closely tied to Collins.[3] The Cork task force contained a similar command balance.

Free State supporters gathered intelligence on Cork defensive preparations throughout July. Though he had relocated to Dublin, Cork TD J. J. Walsh provided some information through his contacts.[4] A more accurate report came from Murt O'Connell, a former Republican prisoner and Gaelic footballer, who apparently worked with local pro-Treaty politicians Maurice O'Connor and Michael Mehigan. This small network was seemingly uncovered by IRA intelligence and its members arrested.[5] A more successful intelligence asset was Mrs Mary Collins-Powell, a sister of Michael Collins. She opened a communications conduit to the British Admiralty, gathered details of the harbour defences, urged commercial leaders to avoid paying taxes and ordered the tax surveyor to flee the city. Most importantly, through the British Legion in Cork, she secured the secret recruitment of up to 700 Cork ex-servicemen into the Free State Army, to be armed after National Army troops landed.[6] This one-woman fifth column ensured that any invading force would receive as much assistance as possible. With her work complete, Collins-Powell conspired with Henry Donegan (one of the city's most prominent Redmondites) to depart Cork secretly aboard a yacht, *The Gull*. Collins-Powell sailed to Waterford and from there continued overland to Dublin, where she reported to her brother. The IRA seem to have been on her trail, however, as *The Gull*'s crew (Donegan, Dr Gerard Ahern and Fr Donal Murphy) were arrested on their return to Crosshaven and detained there until the Free State Army landing a few days later.[7] Despite the importance of Collins-Powell's mission, her brother failed to share the details with Emmet Dalton. The latter subsequently expressed surprise when his erstwhile recruits contacted him on his arrival in Cork.[8]

When conceiving the Cork assault, the National Army antici-pated heavy damage to the city in the fighting. Speaking to a dele-gation of visiting American politicians on 31 July 1922, Michael Collins was philosophical about the potential destruction from the pending attack. When asked whether Cork residents would resent the ruin of their city centre for the second time in two years, 'The General made some reference to the heartlessness of matches, powder and petrol, which know neither remorse nor regret.' He added that 'one of his best friends' commanded the anti-Treaty forces (presumably Liam Lynch).[9] Government propaganda also prepared the public for devastation in Cork. *The Irish People* argued, 'The People of Ireland have to make up their minds as to whether it is better that Cork or the nation be in ruins.' It further con-tended, 'If Cork is in ruins as a result of this struggle, the people will know where to place the responsibility, and it will not be upon the National Government or National Army.'[10]

Vessels for coastal landings were chosen in early July, including the two ships destined for Cork. The *Arvonia* was the larger of the two: 329 feet in length, with three decks and weighing 1,842 tons, while the *Lady Wicklow* had two decks, weighed 1,174 tons and was 260 feet long. The former was operated by the London and North Western Railway and the latter by the British and Irish Steam Packet Company (B&I). Both vessels had shallow drafts and carried wireless transmitters, which made them attractive to the National Army.[11] Their ample cargo space was necessary to carry the men, heavy equipment and hundreds of extra rifles for local recruits. The two vessels formed half of an invasion fleet that was to land in three locations in County Cork in the early morning of 8 August 1922.

Dalton selected 200 men from the Eastern Command to land at Youghal, under the guns of the former HMS *Helga*, recently handed over to the Irish Free State and renamed *Muirchu* to avoid painful memories of Easter 1916. The Youghal force would also carry two armoured cars and an 18-pound field gun. The latter was the standard British army cannon; it possessed a firing range of between 6,000 and 9,000 yards. West of Cork city, another 180 National Army troops with armoured cars were to arrive at Union Hall, near Skibbereen, aboard the B&I vessel *Alexandria*. These two landings were scheduled to begin at 2 a.m., the same time as the main attack on Cork Harbour. When these soldiers were added to those under Dalton's direct command, approximately 830 troops would appear miles behind the IRA front line.

## THE CORK LANDING FORCE

The Cork city landing contingent comprised 450 soldiers from the 2nd Eastern Division of the National Army's Eastern Command. Some came from the Dublin Guards battalion, which had participated in the recent Dublin fighting and was composed of former IRA veterans. General Emmet Dalton later claimed that nearly half of his other soldiers were recruits, with many receiving weapons-training on the boat to Cork.[12] Though Dalton carried numerous armoured cars and artillery (another 18-pound field piece), he still faced formidable Cork Republicans fighting on their home ground. How then did he defeat the IRA in Cork?

When reviewing Dalton's force, its strong leadership cadre stands out. Dalton himself was the finest field commander of the Civil War. Though still only twenty-four years old, he possessed extensive First World War combat experience, having won the Military Cross while still a teenager. He had commanded relatively large bodies of British troops, but also learned guerrilla warfare during his later IRA service. He won fame for the dramatic attempted breakout of Seán MacEoin from Mountjoy Gaol, when he led a disguised IRA squad into and back out of the prison. As the head of IRA training at GHQ, Dalton had even made the personal acquaintance of Cork No. 1 Brigade officers through a training camp visit in 1921. During the critical Free State assault on the Four Courts, Dalton proved to be a calming presence, at one stage operating one of the field guns himself. In the ensuing Cork campaign, he displayed drive and ingenuity, which produced a major victory.[13]

General Tom Ennis served as Dalton's second-in-command. He was an Easter Rising veteran and commanded the Dublin Brigade's 2nd Battalion during the War of Independence. Ennis was an intelligent and charismatic leader, considered by Ernie O'Malley to be, 'the best officer in Dublin'.[14] Reflecting his high level of competence, Ennis was charged with storming the Four Courts, the single most important military operation of the Civil War. Among former Dublin street fighters, Ennis enjoyed perhaps the smoothest transition to conventional army officer.

The third general accompanying the force was a tall, quiet Corkman, responsible for many of the accomplishments attributed to Michael Collins. Major-General Liam Tobin commanded Collins' intelligence department during the War of Independence and now served in a similar capacity in the Free State Army. Tobin also had local contacts in Cork and was probably dispatched to establish a counter-intelligence network there. He was arguably Collins' most trusted subordinate, and one of his deadliest.

Within the landing force, at least three of the senior officers were former members of Michael Collins' famed 'Squad'. Commandant Tom Kilcoyne, Captain Ben Byrne and Commandant Pat McCrea had participated in numerous assassinations and street ambushes. McCrea was the Squad's preferred wheelman, and drove the captured British armoured car in the MacEoin prison escape attempt led by Emmet Dalton. Now commanding the force's armoured vehicles, McCrea personally steered the Rolls-Royce armoured car called 'The Manager'. The three officers each retained a strong personal loyalty to Michael Collins, and could be relied on to fight hard and lead from the front when required.

Two additional officers were critical to the ensuing battle. Peadar Conlon was a combat veteran of the First World War. When he returned to his native Longford, Conlon acted as an IRA intelligence agent, undercover as secretary of the local ex-servicemen's federation. When his activities were discovered, Conlon joined Seán MacEoin's flying column and served as its machine gunner. He was a 'lead magnet', having been wounded in five places while fighting with the IRA and twice more with the Free State Army.[15] Though described by historian Calton Younger as 'a hard and bitter man', the flinty Captain Conlon proved himself a resolute fighter at the exact time when one was needed.[16]

Captain Frank O'Friel had none of the battlefield experience of the other officers. He was a middle-class veteran of the Dublin Brigade, whose brother Henry was a top civil servant in the Irish Free State. O'Friel's importance came from his boyhood spent in the Cork Harbour area, where his father served as the lighthouse keeper at Lahard, Inch, just east of the harbour mouth.[17] As a result of O'Friel's knowledge of the local port and his experience with small boats, he was given a key assignment on the night of the invasion. Once on land, O'Friel performed well as a combat leader, and made a crucial contribution on the second day of fighting.[18]

Beyond its leadership, the Free State force retained other advantages. It had been organised as a formal army for over four months, slowly building up a military administration; it possessed a clear chain of command; its units were structured for battle deployment. Soldiers (usually) wore uniforms, and were armed with rifles that worked and ample ammunition they could trust. When fighting, they were supported by armoured cars, lorries and artillery. The force included a fair number of ex-British army veterans, who provided important leadership at the squad and platoon levels. Though led by former IRA officers, the National Army was designed for conventional warfare, and proved to be much more cohesive and responsive than the IRA. It clearly demonstrated this superiority in the three-day battle fought in the suburbs of Cork city.

## THE LANDING

The *Arvonia* and the *Lady Wicklow* were loaded at the North Wall, Dublin, on the afternoon of Monday 7 August 1922. The *Lady Wicklow* had only docked two days previously, having landed troops at Fenit, County Kerry. On the return trip, the ship carried the bodies of nine National Army soldiers who had been killed in action; their coffins were taken by a guard of honour to Portobello barracks (now Cathal Brugha barracks) and viewed by Michael Collins before a special requiem mass.[19] Boarding troops probably considered these prior passengers with some foreboding.

Security for the operation was lax. Within the Eastern Command, preparations had been ongoing for days. After receiving general absolution from a chaplain at Wellington barracks (later Griffith barracks), departing soldiers were driven in daylight across the city. Armoured cars were moved by crane and manhandled onto the ship's decks. Mattresses tied around cabin windows and sandbags stacked on deck clearly indicated pending action. The

British cabinet was made aware of the operation a few days before it took place. A photographer and two newspaper correspondents accompanying the invasion force must also have been notified in advance.[20] There was even a crowd of cheering well-wishers bidding farewell to the departing troops.[21] In this context, it seems especially negligent that the Dublin Brigade failed to notify IRA headquarters of loaded troopships preparing to sail.

Emmet Dalton intended to enter Cork Harbour, follow the River Lee all the way to Cork and dock at the Ford tractor factory's marina. This pier lay on a peninsula slightly downriver from the city centre, past the point where the north and south channels of the Lee merge. It was only about a quarter of a mile from the Ford factory to the critical bridges crossing the north channel. Dalton could disembark his force and dash across the bridges before the IRA were able to respond. However, Dalton had to change his plan almost immediately after arriving at Cork Harbour.

The two vessels reached the mouth of Cork Harbour at about 1 a.m., with moonlight and lingering twilight providing some relief from the dark sea. The *Lady Wicklow* carried about twenty soldiers and initially acted as a scout ship, running before the packed *Arvonia*. Like any other arrival, the *Arvonia* stopped to take on board a pilot, to guide the ship to its docking destination. The pilot, 25-year-old Joey O'Halloran from Cobh, sensed that something was amiss, even though the troops were hidden below decks. Dalton stood on the bridge and no doubt his Free State Army general's uniform gave the game away. As a Republican, O'Halloran refused to guide the invading force into Cork, citing the Republican dreadnoughts and sea mines upriver. Emmet Dalton responded by pointing a pistol at O'Halloran's head and ordering him to take them as close to Cork as possible. Seeking more reliable navigation assistance from the Royal Navy in Cobh, Dalton wired its flagship HMS *Carysfort*, 'Please send an officer on board'. However, the light cruiser was unaware of the pending operation, and its reply of 'What for?' went unanswered; the *Arvonia* had already proceeded up the channel.[22]

On the bridge of the *Arvonia*, Dalton decided with his officers to make a quick alteration to their plans. Even if his vessels could break through the IRA 'dreadnoughts' upriver, they risked detonating sea mines that had been indicated by Free State Army intelligence and newspaper reports.[23] This was too much of a gamble, even for Dalton, and he sought an alternative landing point. Dalton considered Cobh, but was dissuaded because of the strong IRA defences at Belvelly Bridge. Using Captain O'Friel's harbour expertise, Dalton selected Passage West, located in the narrow river connecting Upper and Lower Harbours, about seven miles from Cork. The town was located well below the Republican river boom and it also contained a dock crane to hoist the heavy armoured cars and artillery piece ashore.[24]

Without delay, the *Arvonia* followed the channel past Cobh, which was occupied by the IRA. Republican sentries hailed the vessel, and shouted questions about its cargo and destination. The *Arvonia* bridge responded evasively as the ship crept past the Republicans, refusing to halt for an IRA powerboat that was sent to investigate. Adding to the IRA confusion was the departure a few hours earlier of the Cork/Holyhead steam packet SS *Classic*, which resembled the inbound vessel; the Republicans seemed reluctant to fire inadvertently on a vessel crowded with passengers. (It is unclear whether the *Lady Wicklow* still accompanied the *Arvonia* at this point, or followed a short time later.)

The suspicious Cobh IRA commander, Mick Burke, called out three IRA patrol cars with Lewis machine guns mounted atop them, from their station at the Rushbrooke shipyard. When the *Arvonia* entered the narrow river connecting Upper and Lower Harbours, the IRA cars kept pace along the river road, with their machine guns trained on the vessel. For the next mile, the Republicans and the *Arvonia* passengers eyed each other tensely across the water, a few hundred metres apart. Though the IRA machine guns endangered his command, Dalton coolly refrained from opening hostilities. He also issued strict orders to the men hidden below deck to ignore any incoming gunfire. As the ship turned towards Passage, a number of warning shots were fired across her bow by both the Cobh and the Passage sentries. At the key moment of the landing operation, the hidden National soldiers aboard the *Arvonia* held their fire. This convinced the Republicans that the *Arvonia* was the *Classic*, returning to port for repairs. Had the soldiers lost their composure, the IRA Volunteers could have delivered deadly machine-gun fire. At that point, the *Arvonia* was also within range of IRA rifle grenades in Cobh, the only weapons with which the Republicans could damage a steel ship. Yet Dalton's luck held.

Alerted to the incoming vessel, the Passage garrison commander summoned the duty guard to the docks and ordered the garrison to turn out. However, still thinking the approaching ship was the *Classic*, the Republicans did not hurry. The *Arvonia* approached the granary quay, but steered clear when a sentry fired a warning shot over her bow. She then glided to a halt at a nearby pier. Before the *Arvonia* eased into a berth, a reconnaissance force composed of Captain Frank O'Friel, General Liam Tobin and twenty soldiers rowed ashore in a lifeboat to ascertain their reception. As the *Arvonia* tied up at the dock, three IRA sentries emerged from the granary headquarters to search the ship, still assuming she was the *Classic*. Carrying a lamp, the leading Republican walked down the pier and started to apologise for the gunfire, then looked up at the deck crowded with troops. He dropped the lantern and dashed into the shadows, as soldiers began to jump onto the pier. Led by General Tom Ennis, they chased the Republicans back to the granary headquarters, which was promptly captured. A newspaper correspondent clocked the docking at exactly 2.20 a.m., and the first troops were ashore two minutes later, on 8 August 1922.[25]

Meanwhile, O'Friel and Tobin's party had landed at the other end of town and worked its way towards the granary. The simultaneous appearance of National Army troops on both sides of town added to the chaos. Shots were exchanged near the pier, killing a Free State soldier and wounding a Republican. A mine on one of the piers may also have been detonated, and confusing gunfire erupted elsewhere in town, but nothing prevented the prompt unloading of 200 soldiers within about ten minutes. By and large, the IRA garrison simply grabbed their weapons and ran away into the darkness. About ten Volunteers were captured around the town. The IRA defenders never used their machine gun and abandoned numerous mines unexploded. Inside the IRA headquarters, Free State soldiers found shotguns, pistols and even shoes and trousers, testifying to the sudden evacuation.

Years later, one of the garrison told Passage historian Colman O'Mahony that they had been shorthanded because of the Bank Holiday, with many men asleep or missing from barracks.[26] This reinforces the impression that, at the most critical location and most critical time, the Cork IRA fielded poorly disciplined, second-rate troops. The Passage Volunteers faced a harsh test late at night on that Bank Holiday Monday; yet the old maxim of 'all's fair in love and war' surely applied here.

Of the two other IRA garrisons attacked simultaneously in County Cork that night, one performed better than Passage and one worse. At Youghal, after the defenders sighted the arriving National Army troops, they set fire to their posts and fled the town, essentially without firing a shot. Across the county at Union Hall, the Free State forces had to row ashore in lifeboats from the *Alexandria* because of IRA's earlier destruction of the landing pier. This extra time allowed the IRA to contest the landing with rifle fire. However, strong machine-gun fire from the *Alexandria* quickly overwhelmed the defenders, just as the Kerry Republicans had been defeated at Fenit the previous week.[27]

The Union Hall experience shows that even a fanatical stand by IRA defenders at Passage armed with eight rifles and a Lewis machine gun would not have stopped 450 Free State soldiers. However, with proper warning they could have inflicted serious casualties before the *Arvonia* landed, and thus demoralised some of the raw National Army troops. Once the vessel docked at Passage, that phase of the battle was already lost. The only question was how easy the victory would be for the National Army. Because of the performance of the Passage IRA, the answer was, very easy.

Once the National Army troops had established a beachhead, they prepared for a quick march into the rebel city. However, they were to find more determined opposition on the road to Cork.

# Chapter 6

# The Battle Begins

The sounds of gunshots, shouts and speeding vehicles aroused some sleeping Cork residents immediately after the Passage landings. However, most people were made aware of the battle by the roar of explosions at 4 a.m. If the IRA defence was initially tardy, there was subsequently no hesitation: within ninety minutes of the National Army troops landing at Passage, a fierce cross-river firefight broke out and bridges began to explode around Cork.

## IRA RESPONSE

Having fled from the Granary headquarters, some IRA defenders regrouped at Clark's Field, on the outskirts above Passage. There they fought back against National Army troops for an hour or so, before completing their retreat from Passage. Though the skirmish caused no casualties, it seems to have slowed the Free State advance, causing the troops to move cautiously in the early morning darkness. The surviving Republicans hustled to Rochestown, where they met gathering IRA Volunteers. One Passage defender needed to be revived and told the attending physician that he had 'run so hard from Passage that his heart had come up into his throat and he wanted some medicine to put it back again'.[1]

Across the river, Cobh Republicans threw themselves into the emerging contest. IRA riflemen took up positions around Carrig-aloe, and began heavy firing on the two ships. Lewis gun bursts soon joined the cacophony of gunfire, 'peppering the troopship'. From the sandbagged decks of the *Arvonia*, National Army troops responded with rifles and machine guns. About 800–900 yards of the River Lee separated the two sides, just on the outer reach of effective rifle fire. 'The shooting was hot and continuous,' wrote one eyewitness; bullets ripped through the seaward sides of both the *Arvonia* and the *Lady Wicklow*, piercing deck doors and the radio rooms, nearly killing the wireless operator on each ship. The *Arvonia* lost the ability to receive radio messages, though the ship could still send them. While the firing disturbed disembarking troops, once ashore they were relatively safe, except for occasional shots from hidden snipers above the town.[2]

At 4 a.m., IRA engineers blew up Fota railway bridge, severing the Cork/Cobh rail line. This seems to have been part of a preconceived defensive response to an anticipated landing in Cobh. Miles away at roughly the same time, the road bridge outside the Rochestown railway station was brought down, cutting the Passage/Cork road. This massive explosion caused serious damage to surrounding buildings. Simultaneously, in the river channel, Republicans scuttled the 'IRA dreadnought', *No. 1 Hopper*. The Republicans took the crew off in a lifeboat (they were left at Blackrock Castle), then detonated a mine in the bilge. The barge sank in the channel, with her funnel peeking through the surface of the water. The other half of the IRA navy, the dredger *Owenabuee*, was left afloat without a crew. When they abandoned the vessel, the Republicans anchored her fore and aft, swinging her across the stream to block the channel. A mine in the bilge was connected by battery cable to the forecastle, but it could not be detonated remotely and so presented little danger to passing craft. Mooring the *Owenabuee* may have been an IRA ruse to dissuade enemies from proceeding up the channel to Cork city. The Cork harbour master was subsequently warned of mines in the river approach to Cork, and the British Admiralty passed the same information on to British shipping lines. Regardless of the IRA's intentions for the remaining blocking ship, Cork city was now isolated by both sea and rail from two possible landing spots. To reach Cork, the National Army troops would have to travel seven miles along the narrow 'Cork road' that hugged Lough Mahon, and proceed through the villages of Rochestown and Douglas.[3]

Republicans from the neighbouring companies of the 2nd Battalion, Cork No. 1 Brigade IRA rallied quickly. At Rochestown and Douglas, local IRA Volunteers were armed mainly with shotguns. Fortunately they had an experienced officer on hand, Peter Donovan, an active gunman and a former commander of the Cork Active Service Unit. Orders came from Cork to fight a delaying action to give the city Volunteers enough time to destroy military installations and remove their supplies. Assembling Republicans set up headquarters at the Rochestown railway station and a defensive post at Rochestown Cross. Other IRA Volunteers assumed sniping positions on the heights overlooking the Passage/Cork road.[4]

In Cork, senior IRA officers scrambled to meet the crisis. At Victoria barracks Sandow O'Donovan gathered all available men and gave them a quick pep talk about the impending combat. When approaching this final hurdle, some Republicans shied away and refused to fight against their countrymen. As for the others, O'Donovan reported that the IRA possessed only thirty-six rifles across the entire city. Armed with these, some Lewis machine guns, shotguns and numerous mines, O'Donovan's scratch force drove south to bolster the Douglas and Rochestown companies. Within the city, largely unarmed Republicans set about destroying military stores. At the Union Quay headquarters, officers burned up the phone lines trying to secure additional reinforcements. City IRA units on the Kilmallock and Waterford fronts were quickly pulled out of the Republican line, and marched towards the nearest railway station. Commandeered trains would carry them forty miles to Cork. It was up to the Republicans at Rochestown to hold back the National Army advance long enough for the IRA reinforcements to arrive.[5]

## THE BATTLE OF DOUGLAS

At Passage, Emmet Dalton divided his force into three skirmishing columns of fifty men each, commanded by Tom Ennis, Tom Kilcoyne and Peadar Conlon. Soon they had established a beachhead of a couple of miles, pushing overland towards Rochestown, as well as west on the Cork road. The troops still had to cope with harassing cross-river fire from the Cobh IRA, but they were in no immediate danger. They may have experienced difficulty with the hoist crane at Passage docks, which delayed the offloading of the armoured cars, but the 18-pound cannon was brought ashore and played a part in the first day's fighting. Later that afternoon, the *Lady Wicklow* returned to Dublin for reinforcements, carrying with her the corpse of the National Army soldier killed a few hours earlier.[6]

Rising above the adjoining villages of Rochestown and Douglas, sloping heights commanded the Cork road. These rolling hills stretched for three miles south towards Carrigaline/Crosshaven, included a number of small woods that provided excellent cover, and were largely unpopulated apart from isolated farms and mansions owned by some of Cork's elite. The Cork road remained impassable as long as the IRA held this area. Most of the serious fighting in the ensuing three-day encounter took place on this extensive high ground, with each side repeatedly seeking to outflank the other. Locally, this combat became known as the Battle of Douglas.

At about noon, National Army troops pushing on towards Rochestown ran into IRA resistance. This evolved into firefights that lasted a number of hours. At this stage, armed Republicans were outnumbered and seriously outgunned, with many carrying shotguns that possessed a fraction of the range and stopping power of a rifle. They did possess machine guns and mines, however, which made up for some of their firepower deficiency.

In Rochestown, the IRA established a string of positions running north to south, anchored by firing posts near the railway station and in homes at the crossroads adjoining the Capuchin Monastery (now Capuchin College). The latter included machine guns placed in two cottages, with firing lines on the ground rising behind them. A wooded glen allowed covered access to the hillside defensive positions to the south towards Oldcourt Wood.

At one of the cottages, a group of about thirty Republicans commanded by Peter Donovan manned the building and surrounding walls. With three machine guns and good ground cover, this was judged to be a sound strongpoint by the newly arrived Cork No. 1 Brigade training officer, Seán Murray. Murray was perhaps the most experienced IRA fighter in mid-Cork. He was a leader of the brigade's flying column in 1921, following extensive First World War combat service with the Irish Guards under the future Field Marshal Harold Alexander of Second World War fame. As the IRA fired from the cottage, Murray watched the National Army troops wheel their 18-pound cannon onto a small hill about 1,000 yards away. He ordered the Republicans to clear the cottage and take shelter among the adjoining hill banks. The field piece then dropped a shell onto the cottage, wrecking the building and raining plaster all over the elderly owner, leaving him shaken but unhurt. His wife emerged to berate the Republicans, shouting, 'It was a misfortunate day when you came along here.' Recognising the absurdity of the situation, Murray 'could only laugh then'.[7] Despite the artillery fire, the IRA still commanded the Cork road, thus stalling the Free State advance.

At 2 p.m. the IRA blew up the Rochestown railway bridge, severing the Cork, Blackrock and Bandon Railway. This prevented the National Army troops at Passage from commandeering a train and riding into the city unopposed. Of even greater concern to the local populace, the long Douglas Channel railway bridge was also brought down, further cutting the railway, as well as the Douglas electric tramway to Cork. For the National Army troops, the city was now directly accessible only by the Cork road.

Obstructed in lower Rochestown and under fire from IRA positions at the nearby Capuchin Monastery, the Free State forces attempted to outflank the Republicans. The National Army troops needed to secure higher ground, so they could get around and above IRA defences on the Cork road. The Republicans attempted to parry these attacks, which resulted in heavy fighting around Oldcourt Wood, between Rochestown and Douglas, about a mile inland. During the afternoon, heavy rifle and machine-gun fire erupted in this warren of fields, woodlands and narrow country lanes.

Deadly encounters took place when the two opposing forces came to grips with each other, sometimes unexpectedly. A group of four Republicans moving through a cottage garden stumbled into a Free State advance group, led by Captain Conlon. The two sides exchanged gunshots at point blank range, with one Republican being killed and two wounded, and two National Army soldiers killed and two wounded, including Conlon. Though Conlon had three fingertips blown off, he wrapped up his hand and continued on with his men. Nearby, another IRA section found itself under fire from both their Republican comrades and National Army troops. Since a few of them were wearing their green Irish Volunteer tunics, the neighbouring Republicans mistook them for National soldiers, and the men hugged the ground as a lead storm broke over them. One Republican, a Royal Navy veteran, claimed the Battle of Jutland, 'was child's play compared to this'.[8] Elsewhere, more confused engagements occurred, though both sides preferred to blaze away from a distance rather than close in on their opponents. IRA engineers placed mines along the roadway to disrupt reinforcements, but these were outflanked by accompanying infantry and were abandoned undetonated.

At about 9 p.m. in the evening, the National Army troops broke into lower Rochestown and seized the railway station. They arrived unexpectedly, probably by working their way around an IRA defensive position. The IRA retreated up the hill slopes in confusion, abandoning a machine gun and other equipment in the process. The Free State forces occupied the station, and commandeered Kelleher's public house as their headquarters. They sandbagged windows and threw up road barricades, converting the area into a stronghold. Relocated to the hills overlooking the Cork road, the Republicans maintained a harassing fire on these forces throughout the night. Occasionally this degenerated into heavy shooting, seemingly coming from all sides. Taking advantage of the darkness, National Army soldiers cleared away some of the wreckage and made the Rochestown Bridge accessible to foot traffic.[9]

Cork No. 1 Brigade reinforcements arrived at the battlefield that evening. The first to appear were about sixty Republicans from the Kilmallock front, who had marched several miles from Bruree to Charleville and boarded a commandeered train for Cork. They pulled into Rochestown at about 6 p.m. and were immediately deployed in ad hoc formations. Dr James Lynch found one of these Republicans wandering alone near his home in Oldcourt, 'absolutely dead to the world'. The exhausted IRA Volunteer told Lynch, 'I am lost. I have not had food for days. I was in Kilmallock last night.' Having recuperated at Lynch's house, the Republican found the rest of his section hiding nearby, with whom he communicated in Irish.[10]

Later in the evening, about eighty Cork Republicans led by Mick Murphy and Pa Murray pulled in. They were among the most experienced fighters in the brigade, and had been holding the Waterford front. When they received word of the Passage landing that morning, they evacuated Dungarvan, commandeered a train, and travelled to Cork via Fermoy, from where lorries brought them to Douglas.[11]

In total, about 140 Republicans arrived in Cork that evening, after travelling roughly forty miles (from Dungarvan or Bruree) in less than a day. That night, the IRA probably fielded at least 200 well-armed Volunteers in jagged lines around Rochestown and Douglas. They also held a large number of unarmed reserves in support. Facing them were an estimated 300 National Army troops in the same confined area. The Cork No. 1 Brigade second team had done its part, preventing a larger and better-armed force from advancing on the city. Emmet Dalton had lost the element of surprise and his troops had failed to advance past Rochestown. The fate of the operation would be decided in a second day of hard fighting.

## IRA DESTRUCTION AND VIEWS FROM THE CITY

Beyond the Rochestown battlefield, IRA engineers were busy across Cork Harbour all day on Tuesday. Republicans from the 9th Battalion destroyed the piers at Ringaskiddy and Currabinny (over the Owenabue River, near Crosshaven and Carrigaline) by setting them alight, while the Ringaskiddy Naval Pier was damaged by flames. Republicans also wrecked the nearby Carrigaline Bridge, and burned the Robert's Cove coastguard station and the naval huts at Crosshaven.

The citizens of Cobh received a rude awakening that morning. At 9 a.m. thick black plumes of smoke rose above the town. Flames appeared from the historic Admiralty House in the town centre, the Belmont naval huts, the naval wireless post (near St Colman's Cathedral), Springfield House and the military hospital located on the eastern edge of town. A spectacular line of fires filled the entire area with smoke and gave the impression of great destruction. In the harbour, the crew of HMS *Carysfort* lined the landside deck, watching the destruction with grim fascination.[12]

Frenzied activity began in Cork at dawn and continued all day. The IRA set up checkpoints at key city intersections, searching for enemy infiltrators and intelligence agents. All the Republican rifles appear to have been sent to Douglas. 'There was a good deal of marching about,' one journalist wrote, 'but I noticed when you saw a body of thirty or forty irregulars on the march, only five or six were carrying firearms.'[13] The Republicans went about seizing vehicles to rescue their stores and supplies. When they commandeered the car driven by the Ford factory manager, Edward Grace, he protested by running up an American flag outside his office. Soon, a small fleet of delivery lorries, motorcycles and private cars was assembled outside the main IRA headquarters at Union Quay, near the ruins of the Carnegie Library, burned down by the Black and Tans in 1920. The Union Quay barracks saw hurried arrivals and departures of messengers, supplies and reinforcements. At one point, an IRA lorry dumped about a hundred bicycles on a street corner, probably to transport arriving Republican troops. Across the river on the South Mall, large crowds of onlookers watched the commotion all day. It seems that most people stayed home from work, thus extending their Bank Holiday. Not knowing whether the city would experience a siege, many residents rushed to buy provisions.[14]

Newspapers reported various notable Republicans directing operations in Cork. Mary MacSwiney and Erskine Childers allegedly ran the Republican headquarters. Éamon de Valera was said to be in the city carrying a rifle. Other newspapers reported his

En route to Cork: National Army armoured cars aboard TSS *Arvonia. (Courtesy of the National Library of Ireland)*

Generals Emmet Dalton (left) and Tom Ennis (right) confer aboard TSS *Arvonia. (Courtesy of the National Library of Ireland)*

National Army troops aboard TSS *Arvonia* apparently return IRA gunfire at Passage. *(Courtesy of the National Library of Ireland)*

In Lough Mahon: the scuttled steamer SS *Gorilla* (foreground) and 'Republican dreadnought' *No. 1 Hopper*. *(Courtesy of the National Library of Ireland)*

Hunting IRA snipers at Passage. *(Courtesy of the National Library of Ireland)*

At Passage docks, disembarking National Army troops prepare to march on Cork. *(Courtesy of the National Library of Ireland)*

Armoured car and troops advance through Passage. *(Courtesy of the National Library of Ireland)*

'Scottie': Ian McKenzie Kennedy, D Company, 8th Battalion, Cork No. 1 Brigade, killed at Rochestown. *(Courtesy of Tony McCarthy)*

*Above and below*: Looting of Victoria barracks. *(Courtesy of the National Library of Ireland)*

IRA Volunteers retreat along the South Mall while withdrawing from the city. *(Courtesy of Gerry White)*

Cheering crowds at Union Quay welcome the first National Army troops into Cork (City Hall in the background). *(Courtesy of the National Library of Ireland)*

Shortly after IRA Volunteers had set fire to their headquarters inside Union Quay RIC barracks. *(Courtesy of Gerry White)*

A National Army post in Emmet Place, following the IRA withdrawal. *(Courtesy of Ken Buckley)*

National Army sentries with Lewis machine guns and armour plating with graffiti, outside the Cork YMCA military post on Marlborough Street. *(Courtesy of Ken Buckley)*

Recently arrived National Army soldiers pose on the Grand Parade, Cork, beside the River Lee. *(Courtesy of Ken Buckley)*

presence on the Kilmallock front, accompanied by both Childers and Bob Barton. Childers had apparently been near Kilmallock at the time of the landing, but returned to Cork to evacuate his Republican publicity department. Frank O'Connor later saw him on the Western Road during the evacuation of the city, merrily waving from the running board of a speeding lorry.[15]

Elsewhere in the city, Republican squads targeted the *Cork Examiner* and *Cork Constitution* newspapers, each owned by outspoken public opponents. At noon, about forty men with sledgehammers and revolvers entered the *Examiner* office. When the staff refused to leave, shots were fired over their heads to force them outside. IRA Volunteers then systematically smashed up the printing presses, causing £39,000 worth of damage. A similar group went on to the *Constitution* and created another £23,000 worth of destruction.[16]

The scale and danger of events became apparent in the early evening, when smoke rose from Victoria barracks, atop the highest hill of the city. The temporary huts inside were fired, probably to facilitate the final burning of the barracks. Large drums of petrol had been positioned outside the buildings before the invasion. The Republicans also drove the Cork Fire Brigade tender and steam engine to Ballincollig barracks, to forestall any effort to save Victoria. (A firefighter accompanied them and recovered the hoses and pipes; the other equipment was returned wrecked two days later.)[17] Huge clouds of black smoke hung over the city: 'The fire lit up the entire sky and greatly alarmed everybody,' wrote one impressed journalist.[18]

The Associated Press sensationally and erroneously reported that St Patrick's Street and the Imperial Hotel had been burned to the ground; *The New York Times* claimed that the city had suffered £2,000,000 worth of damage, the city centre was 'in ruins', and Republican snipers in the rubble were terrorising the population.

More *bona fide* property damage befell Government House, home to the military commander of the Victoria barracks. Anticipating the burning of the building, looters descended on the ornate mansion and removed all the furniture and fittings, including an impressive stone fireplace and an enormous porcelain bath, the latter being driven off in a small donkey cart.[19]

The sounds of heavy gunfire and occasional artillery rounds were audible in the city all day. The crowds on the South Mall departed in the evening. Some must have noticed the new Republican sniper post on the roof of the Cork Savings Bank, which suggested that the IRA would bring the fight into the city itself. Wreckage, destruction and economic ruin seemed to be imminent. Cork citizens could only speculate as to what the next day would bring.

# CHAPTER 7

# THE BATTLE RAGES

Having failed to make a quick march on Cork during Tuesday, the National Army troops came to grips with the Republicans on Wednesday 9 August, resulting in some of the most intense combat of the Civil War. However, the Rochestown area was not the only part of Cork to experience extraordinary events that day.

## WAR ON THE WATER

From the outset of the Passage landings, the Port of Cork faced severe challenges from cross-channel firing, the IRA river boom and suspected channel mines. On Tuesday at 7 a.m., only a few hours after the landing, the potential for disaster was illustrated by the Belfast steamer, SS *Orlock Head*. Arriving from Antwerp, the *Orlock Head* steamed up the channel towards Cork, unaware of the bullets flying between Carrigaloe and Passage. Only at the last moment did the crew detect the cross-river shooting and turn the vessel around.[1] A few hours later, the Cork Harbour Commissioners' Dredge and Works Committee meeting was interrupted dramatically by the news that the Republicans had scuttled a ship in the river channel. The harbour master and board chairman rushed immediately to the IRA headquarters to ascertain whether vessels could continue to service the port.[2] The officials had to balance the financial consequences of closing the port against their responsibility for the safety of the vessels using it.

Captain Hugh Somerville, commanding the Royal Navy forces at Haulbowline, decided to take matters into his own hands. A west Cork resident and brother of writer Edith Somerville, Captain Somerville recognised the need to play down British support of the Irish Free State government. Receiving word of the blocked river channel on Tuesday morning, Somerville gathered up Captain Alfred Carpenter, who commanded HMS *Carysfort* and won a Victoria Cross in 1918 for the Zeebrugge raid. In the *Carysfort*'s launch, the two officers motored upriver to the moored *Owenabuee*, presumably bypassing the Carrigaloe gunfire. Aboard the Republican dreadnought, they disconnected a cable running to a mine below deck, and cast off the stern anchor, which allowed the ship to swing with the tide and thus clear the channel. The two officers returned to Passage to inform General Dalton that the channel was no longer obstructed and his ships could proceed to Cork. When he arrived back at Haulbowline, Somerville dispatched a naval tug to collect the *Owenabuee*. The tug was fired on by IRA Volunteers but not hit, and it towed the dredger safely to Lower Harbour. Somerville moored the vessel alongside the monitor HMS *Severn*, had the mine removed, and later returned the ship to the Cork Harbour Board with his compliments and a bill. Sensitive about appearances, Somerville charged the Harbour Board £18.14 for the Royal Navy's services, an amount the board gladly paid.[3]

The Republicans did not take Somerville's intervention lying down. About midday on Wednesday 9 August, they arrived at Cork's Customs House Quay and boarded the SS *Gorilla* – a new, 772-ton steamer, built earlier that year by Belfast's Harland and Wolff for G. & J. Burns of Glasgow. The Republicans took the ship down the channel to the spot where they had sunk the dredging barge *No. 1 Hopper*, and scuttled it. However, the tide subsequently pushed the sunken vessel further towards the shore, leaving a 200-foot gap in the channel. The channel thus remained navigable, but dangerous, and vessels had to proceed with caution over the coming weeks. The *Gorilla* was subsequently raised and repaired at the end of the month. This quick salvage indicates a lack of major structural damage to the vessel, which would be consistent with scuttling by opening the ship's valves rather than through an explosion.[4]

Also on Wednesday, another ship entered the cross-channel firing line: SS *City of Dortmund*, formerly an IRA gun-running steamer, arrived from Antwerp unaware of the hostilities upriver. Near Passage and Carrigaloe, bullets peppered the ship, causing passengers to dive for cover. The two sides eventually held their fire, agreed to a one-hour ceasefire, and signalled the *City of Dortmund* to proceed. Rattled but safe, the steamer arrived in Cork without further harm.[5]

A stubborn section of Cobh Republicans kept the Passage docks under fire for the duration of the fighting at Douglas and Rochestown. Their shooting eventually drove the National Army troops to respond with artillery on Wednesday afternoon. Shells landed around the IRA headquarters at Fota House, apparently causing Republican casualties who had to be treated in Cork. The firing resumed afterwards, and the Cobh Republicans maintained their positions until ordered to evacuate on Friday 11 August. One Carrigaloe homeowner subsequently claimed compensation for the destruction caused to his home and furniture by gunfire. Though the Cobh Volunteers pinned a small force of National Army troops at Passage to defend the docks, the Republicans here largely engaged in a fruitless exercise.

The failure to better deploy a well-armed IRA unit illustrates the lack of imagination of Cork No. 1 Brigade OC Mick Leahy. Conditioned by guerrilla warfare to defer to local initiative and new to the command of a brigade, Leahy exercised a loose leadership. Throughout the fighting, he appeared to co-ordinate the

Republican response rather than direct it. In turn, his superiors, Liam Deasy and Liam Lynch, made no effort to interfere with Leahy's control of the battle. This contrasted starkly with the hierarchical Free State Army, whose decisive leaders proved to be much more effective.[6]

## THE FIGHTING RESUMES

Along and above the Cork road at daybreak on Wednesday 9 August, shooting erupted and then grew even more intense. Fighting continued up and down a rough front line that included Rochestown, Monfieldstown and Oldcourt, extending about two miles across broken country and the slopes overlooking Lough Mahon. Rifles and machine guns blasted away at each other, while Free State artillery also came into play.

The crossroads adjoining the Capuchin Monastery became a contested battlefield. Amid the intense gunfire, the two sides closed on each other and some hand-to-hand combat reportedly took place. Most notably, west Cork National Army soldier Michael Collins (a cousin of the commander-in-chief) charged a Republican machine gun, but his pistol jammed. Collins tried to wrest the machine gun away from the gunner, but he received a point-blank burst fired through his lower body. His wounds proved fatal after he lingered for several days in a Cork hospital.

In Douglas, west of Rochestown, the IRA used Maryborough Hill and the Douglas Golf Club as assembly areas. On the lawn in front of Maryborough House, Republicans exchanged fire with National Army troops on an opposing hill.[7] Others fought it out around Thomas O'Grady's house in Monfieldstown. Republican defenders were occasionally shelled out of positions, or driven out by Free State armoured cars, most notably 'The Manager'. However, the IRA lines refused to buckle, and the Cork road remained closed to National Army troops.

In the early afternoon, Captain Peadar Conlon and twenty-five men arrived at Dr James Lynch's house in Garryduff. They had pushed west from Passage across the high ground well above Rochestown, reaching the southern flank of the Republican line. Conlon proceeded to establish his base in the Lynch home, posting a machine gun upstairs and deploying his men around the outbuildings and ditches. Shortly after Conlon's arrival, Dr Lynch noted the appearance of a suspected freebooter, who walked upstairs allegedly to site a machine gun for the National Army. When Lynch questioned the stranger, he advised the doctor and his family to flee as the Republicans were expected to arrive shortly. The man departed abruptly after Lynch referred him to Captain Conlon. He was only one of many opportunists around Cork who used the chaos to their own advantage.[8]

Republicans on a nearby rise opened fire on Conlon's men, then redeployed for better shooting angles. Lynch's house was largely spared in the ensuing firefight, which the doctor attributed to a promise he had received from Republicans after he treated their wounded comrade the previous day; Lynch had asked them to avoid the house and his family inside it. Though the Lynch house received little fire, IRA bullets sprayed the outbuildings, and Lynch saw at least one National Army soldier fall. Lynch recalled Conlon shouting above the roar of the shooting, 'Well, I am damned! But it is madness.'[9]

By this time, Emmet Dalton had changed tactics. Stymied by the Republicans above the Cork road, Dalton mobilised his reserves at the Passage docks and sent them forward in the afternoon. Captain Frank O'Friel and his platoon represented one part of a Free State pincer movement. They were dispatched to Rochestown, with orders to follow Monastery Road south to Belmont House, near Dr Lynch's house. Tom Kilcoyne's force was tasked with doubling back east towards Passage, circling around the Republican positions, and attacking from the south and west to reunite with O'Friel's troops. For unknown reasons, Kilcoyne did not close his end of the encirclement quickly enough, which left O'Friel vulnerable. As he pushed forward in the late afternoon, O'Friel led his men into a turnip field, unaware that it was covered by an IRA machine gun. Gunfire killed five soldiers, as well as a heifer and a bull. Hugging the ground, O'Friel and his men backed out of danger. Shortly afterwards, O'Friel knocked on the door of Dr Lynch's house. The doctor recalled that O'Friel was, 'so plastered with mud and blood from head to foot that he was quite unrecognisable'.[10]

O'Friel combined his force with Conlon's just as the Republicans counter-attacked. O'Friel had only just sat down to revive himself when word came to Lynch's house that their soldiers were in full flight. Conlon shouted, 'The day is lost', and grabbed O'Friel and Dr Lynch to head off the panicked troops. Taking a shortcut, they beat their men to Barrett's cottage, and rallied them on the road there. Lynch remembered the two officers, 'sprinting up the centre, their revolvers pointed at their men and calling on them to right about face'.[11] When the panic had subsided, the two sides squared off again, with National Army soldiers at Barrett's cottage facing Republicans at William Cronin's cottage on higher ground at Ballincurrig crossroads, Moneygurney. During the intense firefight, rifles and machine guns blazed away freely. According to one resident, the gunfire was 'simply terrifying'. Lynch recalled pressing his face into the ground: 'There was a hail of berries on me from the trees above as the bullets riddled them from side to side.' He subsequently treated a wounded Republican machine-gunner who told him he had been in the act of pulling the trigger on Lynch and a group of soldiers when he was shot in the back.[12]

By 5 p.m. the exchange had become 'intense and practically incessant'.[13] This seemed to herald the closing of the National Army troops' pincer movement, as Tom Kilcoyne's detachment came around the Republican flank. With the National Army soldiers threatening to enfilade the IRA line, the Republicans apparently chose to cede the high ground. IRA Volunteers began to fall back from their firing positions to waiting lorries. Covering their retreat were three determined Republicans posted inside Cronin's cottage.[14]

The rearguard was led by one of the most colourful characters in the Republican ranks, Ian MacKenzie Kennedy, fondly known as 'Scottie' to the Cork No. 1 Brigade. Supposedly a linear descendant of Robert the Bruce, MacKenzie Kennedy was brought from Scotland to Ireland by his mother, to save him from dangerous military service in the First World War. A devoted bagpiper and Irish language student, MacKenzie Kennedy settled in Ballyvourney and promptly joined D company, 8th Battalion, Cork No. 1 Brigade. He was genuinely popular among his neighbours and comrades, if a frequent source of kilted amusement. Among other eccentricities, he attached a small sail to his bicycle, experimented with home-made explosives and attempted to engineer a giant spring trap to knock down police barrack doors.[15] 'Tall, fairhaired, and boyishly handsome,' was how one female contemporary remembered him. 'He was charming and so wonderful to look at.'[16] 'He was a grand character and a good fighter,' recalled City IRA veteran George Gunn, 'of course we never thought he was a fighter because he used to go around in his kilts, like.'[17]

From the kitchen of Cronin's cottage, 'Scottie' and his two comrades kept up a heavy fusillade against the National Army troops. A squad of soldiers attempted to storm the house, with Peadar Conlon leading from the front, as usual. Poised outside the kitchen doorway, Conlon called on the Republicans to surrender. They answered with a shotgun blast through the doorjamb, shooting Conlon's face full of pellets in what seemed to be a mortal wound. According to Free State sources, National troops tossed grenades into the cottage and shot down MacKenzie Kennedy and James Moloney as they dashed from the side door. Republicans claimed both were killed walking from the cottage with their hands up, 'cut in two' by a machine gun. Dr Lynch found their bodies sprawled across the lane in 'a lake of blood'. Testifying to the severity of the fight, *The Cork Examiner* reported of the cottage, 'Hundreds of bullets entered and tore walls and furniture.'[18]

A further Free State advance was foiled by the onset of darkness and the reappearance of what Frank O'Connor dubbed ironically 'our particularly fierce armoured car', 'The River Lee'. It stalked the back lanes near Ballincurrig Cross, putting the National Army troops on edge, though an impromptu road barricade kept the so-called 'labourer's cottage' at bay. Despite this, Emmet Dalton must have been satisfied with the evening's battle. Now commanding high ground overlooking the north and the west, National Army troops could fire down on IRA defensive positions. Though only used a few times, the 18-pound artillery piece forced the Republicans to abandon posts that were impervious to bullets but not cannons.[19]

Rather than form a new defensive line closer to Cork, the Republicans simply held their ground with little direction from their command. To IRA Volunteers fed into the fighting, such as Jamie Moynihan, 'it was all panic ... there was no order then'. The Republicans were 'all up in a heap', recalled George Gunn, 'a very great confusion'. Frank Busteed claimed that his column experienced 'complete disorganisation'. He phoned Union Quay barracks repeatedly for reinforcements, but the Cork No. 1 Brigade could not provide them. To the brigade vice-commander, Sandow O'Donovan, there was 'no organisation in Cork'.[20] Events simply moved too quickly for the Republican leadership to respond. They had no support services, few reserves and limited arms and ammunition. Most of their column fighters served in ad hoc units formed on a largely voluntary basis. The Republican army's decentralised composition and flat command structure made a fight on this kind of scale nearly impossible to manage. Though the Cork Republicans fought stubbornly, their system of organisation ultimately prevented them from waging conventional warfare in the cohesive and sustained manner required in Douglas/Rochestown.

Despite these shortcomings, IRA chief of staff Liam Lynch took heart that the Free State forces had 'made scarcely any progress towards Cork City'. However, he still anticipated returning to guerrilla tactics within the next week or two. For Lynch, the Republicans' primary mission was to preserve themselves as a fighting force, rather than to keep the National Army troops out of Cork. This conservative outlook was a critical factor in the events of the following day.[21]

Returning from the battle to his home (now a first aid station), Dr Lynch was relieved to see Captain Conlon sitting in an armchair, casually smoking a cigarette despite the pellet wounds on his face. The Longford man seemed impervious to both bullets and jibes from Lynch's children, who called him 'raspberry jam' owing to the shotgun wounds. According to Lynch, Conlon was the real hero of the recent fighting. 'He was a born leader, absolutely fearless and possessed an extraordinary animal magnetism,' said the snobbish Lynch, 'although he had not taken a university degree.'

Lynch reported providing meals for between 80 and 100 National Army troops that night, and 120 the next morning. Scores of soldiers slept outside his home and all along the roadways. Their slumber was not disturbed by the arrival of Generals Emmet Dalton and Tom Ennis at 3 a.m. Their opponents were even more exhausted; the Republican reinforcements 'had been line fighting for weeks and they had been brought back without sleep'. They collapsed for a more fitful rest that summer night.[22]

The intensity of the fighting was confirmed by the great number of casualties treated. Inside Dr Lynch's home, wounded soldiers lay bleeding in his hallway, drawing-room, dining-room and pantry. That night, Lynch claimed to have attended to thirty wounded men, from both sides, in his makeshift hospital. The house was so crowded that they had to seek additional accommodation. Conlon colourfully ordered a subordinate to 'Take ten men with rifles; tell them to take any home Dr Lynch says; to shoot anyone Dr Lynch tells them to – and to clear the blazes of this, for I want to sleep.' With Lynch leading the way, the soldiers commandeered the house of his neighbour, land agent William Clarke, to act as a second dressing station.[23]

Clarke's young granddaughter recalled seeing wounded men lying on mattresses in the dining-room and along the hallway. On horseback, she later rode through the IRA lines, and watched the Republicans struggling to cope with the casualties. Of particular fascination was an overloaded Thompson's bread van carrying dead and wounded Republicans. 'Its springs were down on the axles with one flat tyre and steam coming out of its radiator,' she recalled. As it went uphill, an IRA Volunteer jogged behind it to hold the rear doors closed:

> Never, as long as I live, will I forget the pitiful, anguished sight of that van … The carnage of battle was strewn about, bloody rags, pools of blood on the road, the remains of old Leyland lorries lay dumped and crumpled in the ditches, the cottages, their roofs of slate or thatch riddled with bullets, their windows staring like blind eyes where they had been machine-gunned out.[24]

*The Irish Times* reported that fourteen wounded from both sides were treated in the *Arvonia*'s saloon. Other casualties were taken to Cork hospitals by boat, including one wounded National soldier who misheard his Rochestown location and thought he was in Punchestown, near Dublin.[25] On the Republican side, a dozen Cumann na mBan nurses headed for the battlefield on Wednesday evening, along with a number of small, convertible motor cars fitted to carry stretchers.[26] City ambulances collected corpses, and some of the dead were laid out in local mortuaries.[27] Six National Army privates killed on 8 August were later returned via boat to their home city of Dublin.[28]

Total casualties from the encounter are difficult to ascertain. Some available data refers only to the second day of fighting, while other data relates to the full three-day battle. In the entire operation, Emmet Dalton reported suffering ten dead and twelve wounded men, against twenty-five dead and thirty-five wounded for the Republicans. His wounded total seems too low compared to his fatalities (it might only account for those requiring hospitalisation), while the IRA losses are not reflected in Cork No. 1 Brigade death rolls. Dr Lynch's count of thirty-five killed and seventy-five wounded combined on both sides appears to be inflated, though his service as the National Army's medical officer during the fight adds a certain credibility. Various newspapers reported Republican casualties as between six and nine dead, and twenty to thirty wounded.[29] The reliable historian, Colman O'Mahony, names seven Republican fatalities, which matches a separate account that includes an eighth name.[30] Carefully qualified, my estimate runs to a combined seventeen to twenty-five killed during the three days (at least ten Free State soldiers and seven Republicans), and another thirty to sixty wounded, from both sides. The only thing we can be sure of is that a large number of men were killed at Douglas/Rochestown and an even larger number wounded. The impact on civilians seemed limited to property damage and a good fright.

That evening in Cork, IRA Volunteers began packing up supplies and seizing equipment, food and office supplies. Anticipating Republican raids, the city banks refused to cash bank drafts and notes, and shut their doors for the week; most shops and businesses also closed.[31]

The fighting had moved noticeably closer to Cork, with gunfire and booming artillery now louder, and clearly coming from the city's southern suburbs. On the South Mall, hundreds gathered as if on a vigil, searching for signs indicating the fate of their city. Would the Republicans fight within the crowded city centre? Could critical buildings withstand Free State artillery? Would flames engulf entire neighbourhoods? How many more would die in this unpopular Civil War? In that long summer twilight, answers seemed within earshot but out of sight. Down the road a few miles, the city's future was being decided.

# CHAPTER 8

# THE BATTLE ENDS

The fighting resumed early on Thursday 10 August, but did not approach the intensity of the previous day. On Wednesday, Republicans sat atop Maryborough Hill in command of the Cork road. On Thursday, they were driven from the position by Free State artillery and armoured-car machine guns firing from the high ground captured the previous day. Artillery was also used against another IRA concentration near the Ravenscourt mansion. Once the Republicans were cleared from the heights overlooking the Cork road, National Army troops and armoured cars pushed into Douglas village.

Limited fighting occurred in Douglas village, as accurate Republican riflemen from Rectory Hill harassed National Army troops working their way forward. Another firefight broke out around the Fingerpost roundabout. Locals seemed to have warned both sides when they were entering a dangerous area. George Gunn credited a young girl with leading his IRA squad away from a Free State ambush at the gate of Maryborough House. Returning to the fight, the seemingly indestructible Peadar Conlon was reportedly saved by an elderly woman, who waved his patrol away as they walked into a Republican fire zone. The Free State armoured car, 'The Manager', was involved in an almost comical car chase with an IRA lorry. Unclear as to the way to Cork, 'The Manager' stopped at O'Driscoll's pub to ask for directions. At the same moment, a lorry filled with Republicans nosed around the corner and saw 'The Manager'. The lorry promptly reversed itself, spun around and hightailed it for a small bridge near O'Brien's Mills that was ready for demolition. Pursued by 'The Manager', the Republicans crossed the bridge, which was promptly blown up behind them.[1]

The Free State forces kept up the pressure as they advanced through Douglas. Their armoured cars cut off some Republicans on the high ground, while other IRA Volunteers could not withstand the firepower directed towards them. Frank Busteed remembered barricading himself and another senior IRA officer inside a cottage, while a nearby companion had his hand shot off. Owing to 'very severe firing' recalled IRA leader Connie Neenan, 'we had no choice but to retreat along the Douglas Road'. Before the Republicans fell back, they opened a road trench that may well have slowed the National Army troops.[2]

The Republicans had already decided to withdraw from the city on Thursday morning. The order probably came from Cork No. 1 Brigade OC Mick Leahy, with the approval of the 1st Southern Division commander, Liam Deasy. Their motivation seems to have been to spare the civilian population the hardship of protracted city fighting. The Republicans subsequently burned down a few structures they deemed to be of military value (police and army barracks), but largely left the city as they had found it. The day of the withdrawal, Liam Lynch sent instructions to Cork No. 1 Brigade cancelling the planned destruction of the Cork Customs House, and suggesting that the Republicans return the Cork Fire Brigade equipment sent to Ballincollig, 'in the event of a serious fire breaking out' in the city. He further advised against burning the Bridewell (police headquarters) as it adjoined a timber yard that might catch fire and cause widespread destruction. While Lynch was aware of the importance of retaining popular support for the IRA, this policy stopped when it came to the destruction of roads, bridges and railways. To paralyse Free State troops, he ordered the Republicans to disable Cork's infrastructure on a massive and thorough scale, despite the severe damage it would cause the local economy.[3]

## REPUBLICAN RETREAT

In the early morning of 10 August, IRA engineers blew up part of the Chetwynd railway viaduct (Cork, Bandon and South Coast Railway), about two miles south-west of the city on the Bandon road; they also wrecked the Rathpeacon viaduct north of Cork, thereby severing the Great Southern and Western Railway.[4] These were by no means the only bridges attacked in the coming hours.

At Victoria barracks, the Republicans marched 200 Free State prisoners-of-war from the Cork barracks to Blarney, about five miles away. As they passed a concerned elderly woman, one prisoner shouted, 'It's all right, mother, we will be marching them tomorrow.' At Blarney, the Republicans removed the prisoners' shoes and released them. Because of the collapse of transportation in the south, 140 former POWs were housed at the Cork Asylum over the next four nights.[5]

By late morning, IRA Volunteers had prepared fall-back positions in large buildings along the South Mall (adjoining the south channel of the River Lee), to cover their comrades retreating from Douglas. Firing posts were established on top of the Cork Provincial Bank and Cork Savings Bank; the Republicans also seized the Imperial Hotel, the County Club, the Ex-Servicemen's Club and McDonnell's Corn Merchants, 92 South Mall. In the latter premises, Volunteers barricaded the windows with sacks of cornmeal, and tunnelled through the walls to connect with Oliver Plunkett Street. At the Cork Ex-Servicemen's Association rooms, a disturbance broke out, apparently as the ex-soldiers defended their headquarters from possible destruction. The Republicans fired some shots over the heads of the ex-servicemen, seemingly scattering them. However, with salvation now at hand, other ex-soldiers worked to assist the approaching National Army troops. They sabotaged the Cork phone lines, making communication even more difficult for the IRA.[6]

The Republican withdrawal began calmly enough. In Douglas, IRA Volunteers disengaged at about midday and tried to move out of the city before the National Army troops appeared. However, the National Army's rapid advance through Douglas seems to have made IRA leaders believe that their opponents would enter Cork before their evacuation was complete.

At Union Quay barracks, Mick Murphy found, 'everything was pretty chaotic there'. For engineer Eamon Enright, 'The Staters were not expected so soon and there was a panic.' The writer Frank O'Connor dramatically recalled his visit to Union Quay: 'There was a crowd of bewildered men in the roadway outside and a senior officer was waving his arms and shouting: "Every man for himself".' At the other Republican headquarters at 56 Grand Parade, Geraldine Neeson of Cumann na mBan reported, 'Everybody was busy, sorting papers, burning documents, shouting orders, trying to use the telephone and rushing up and downstairs.' She was handed a jar of glycerine and told to hide it; Neeson discreetly left it in a priest's confessional at Ss Peter and Paul's church.[7]

Elsewhere, IRA Volunteers drove around the city seizing useful items for their field army. Typewriters and a rotary stencil machine were commandeered from the Corporation; at the Cork Wireless School, Republicans secured a radio transmitter and other equipment. Military supplies were loaded into waiting lorries. These included food, ammunition and explosives, but also bomb workshop materials, printing presses and communications equipment. Scores of lorries and cars waited to begin the retreat west to Macroom. Elsewhere, IRA Volunteers destroyed the telegraph office at the General Post Office, as well as the telephone exchange on MacCurtain Street.[8]

At about noon, retreating Republican troops began to cross the south channel bridges on foot. Weary but in good military order, they marched up the South Mall and assembled in the Grand Parade and Cornmarket Street. IRA Volunteers from Kerry and west Cork were to withdraw to Macroom, along with columns from the 7th (Macroom) and 8th (Ballyvourney) Battalions. Specialist units such as engineers, signallers, chemicals and administrative staff would similarly fall back to Macroom. However, local fighters were ordered to march about ten miles north to the Donoughmore area, which provided good cover. These included sections from the 1st (Cork City), 2nd (Cork City), 3rd (Ballincollig), 5th (Riverstown/Whitechurch) and 6th (Blarney/Donoughmore) Battalions.[9]

Retiring from Douglas to Cork, Republican George Gunn recalled that he and his comrades 'looked horrible'. A member of a Cork City column, Gunn had changed his clothing only once in six weeks of combat service, and had eaten nothing during two days of fighting. In Cork, he found residents were generous: 'The people were very good; they felt sorry for us.' In Douglas, a woman gave Gunn and his companions a bucket of eggs; at George's Quay in Cork, another woman handed them all the coins she carried. While they rested at Coal Quay, neighbours served them lemonade. Yet the defeat was utterly demoralising. Marching up the South Mall, one Republican shouted to a pedestrian, 'We are going home! We are beaten. We are fed up.'[10]

With their battered trench coats, caps, ammunition bandoleers and slung rifles, scores of Republicans marched wearily out of Cork. They trudged down Washington Street and Western Road, while others moved along Blarney Street and Sunday's Well Road towards Clogheen. Along Western Road, residents stood at their doorways to watch the depressed procession. Tired of walking, some Republicans commandeered the Muskerry Tram, a light railway that ran all the way to Donoughmore. The tram occasionally stopped for more Republicans to board, as if they were commuters returning home after a particularly bad day at the office.[11]

Once again, hundreds of Cork residents gravitated to the South Mall, across the river from Union Quay barracks. The intersection provided a direct view of the IRA headquarters, and was also where Douglas Road fed into the city via Anglesea Street and Parnell Bridge. National Army troops would probably enter Cork at this spot. Within hours, thousands of citizens were watching events from here.

At about 2 p.m. military posts across the city were set alight. These had already been prepared for destruction, with large barrels of oil positioned in each structure. Motorcycle messengers delivered the destruction order to each location: Empress Place police barracks (commandeered by the Auxiliary cadets in 1920), Cat Fort, Elizabeth Fort (the wooden building inside), Bridewell station, Shandon barracks and Tuckey Street barracks. Residents of adjoining homes and shops fled with whatever they could carry, fearing that the flames would spread into their properties. Despite the risk, however, all the fires remained confined to the targeted buildings. Danger came from elsewhere at Tuckey Street, where two Republicans sleeping on the second floor awoke to find the barracks in flames. Panicking, they prepared to jump from a window, but were calmed by a gathering crowd who provided a long rescue ladder. The Republicans escaped, singed but otherwise unhurt. A similar incident occurred at Ballincollig barracks, but in this case, a sleeping IRA Volunteer, Patrick Burns, suffered fatal injuries. Both episodes illustrate the rushed nature of this destruction as well as the physical exhaustion of IRA troops.[12]

Victoria barracks produced the biggest blaze, as its remaining headquarter buildings, sleeping quarters and military hospital went up in flames. Neighbours felt the intense heat and were rattled by small explosions, apparently from barrack chimneys booby-trapped by former British army occupants.[13]

Giant plumes of black smoke rose across the city, giving the impression of even greater destruction. An *Irish Independent* correspondent in Cork wrote:

> Like the waters of many rivers converging into a big lake, the smoke of many fires has converged into one dense mass which hangs like a deadly pall over the whole city. The air below, as it were, is imprisoned, and one stifles with the heat, and the acrid smell of burning buildings. The sun is darkened; one can see through the smoke, a red, almost a bloody, disc. Showers of charred papers and other debris are falling everywhere, and litter the streets.[14]

A Free State Air Corps biplane buzzed the city. It reported, 'One would imagine to see Cork City from the air that the whole town was enveloped in flames. Closer examination revealed the fact that all barracks, police and military, were on fire.' The Bristol fighter had been tasked with reporting on conditions, strafing Republican formations and dropping thousands of Free State Army propaganda leaflets. Flying in from Waterford, the plane circled the city for some time before proceeding to Midleton, where it made several strafing runs on Republicans who had fired at it. The Bristol failed to achieve its final mission, however, which was to drop a message to Dalton's command assuring them that their wireless messages were being heard in Dublin. The plane tossed the message towards Passage docks, but it missed its target and fell into the river. Dalton remained cut off from his Dublin headquarters.[15]

At about 3 p.m. Republican vehicles started their retreat to Macroom. Scores of lorries sped through Cork packed with war supplies and IRA Volunteers. Some Republicans stood on running boards, while others held on to rear doors. The strange convoy included commercial delivery lorries, private cars, Corporation refuse carriers, motorcycles and even bicycles. Curious residents remained at their doorways watching vehicle after vehicle race down Western Road.

## EVACUATION

At about 4 p.m. the final evacuation began, as Union Quay barracks saw a last spell of activity. The Republicans there found themselves with about a dozen damaged vehicles that were impossible to move. Rather than let them fall into Free State hands, they dumped the lorries, cars and motorcycles into the river in front of the barracks. Now packed like a gallery, the South Mall offered front row viewing as the Republicans wheeled a lorry to the edge of the channel. 'They push it into the river,' read a correspondent's notes, 'another and another and another. And yet another meet [*sic*] with similar fate before the horrified gaze of the crowd.' The axle of one car caught on the pier and hung there for a long moment, before it too dropped into the water.[16]

Thousands on the South Mall witnessed the IRA's grand finale: the burning of Union Quay barracks. To prevent the fire from being extinguished, Republicans cut adjoining water mains and moved Cork Fire Brigade equipment from the nearby Sullivan Quay station. When it came time to set the blaze, onlookers and potential looters gathered outside the building. Riflemen on top of the Cork Savings Bank fired warning rounds over their heads, while other Republicans shot their pistols into the air to finally clear the street. The building caught fire quickly; by the time the last IRA Volunteers crossed the south side of the river channel,

Union Quay barracks was belching thick smoke. Pops of exploding ammunition gave way to disturbing booms from grenades missed in the evacuation. The enthralled crowd stood their ground despite repeated detonations, which were powerful enough to shatter all the windows on Morrison's Quay and the Provincial and Savings Banks on the South Mall.[17]

Now safely across the southern river channel, IRA engineers sought to slow the Free State pursuit. The Clontarf railway draw-bridge was drawn up, and control panel parts removed to lock the span in the open position. At Parliament Bridge, an 1806 city landmark, the engineers detonated a landmine, probably intending to block the roadway rather than to collapse the bridge. Finally, the engineers rigged another mine on the Parnell Bridge, directly in front of the South Mall crowds. This 'terrific explosion' ripped one of the girders into 'lattice-work', though again the roadway suffered the most. One witness testified, 'a piece of this girder flew 100 yards and smashed Mr Paine's bicycle as he was watching the fun'.[18]

Along the South Mall, a string of Republican scouts watched for approaching troops. Lorries kept their engines running, while officers checked the city centre for stragglers. Satisfied that there was nothing more to be done, they issued the final withdrawal order to the South Mall scouts. The scouts relayed it to each other, one by one down the long street, before each turned and jogged away. The last vehicles sped out of Cork around 5 p.m. on Thursday 10 August, thus ending the Republican control of the city.

Once residents were satisfied the Republicans had gone, looting began. Initially the burning barracks were targeted, despite the heat and exploding ordnance. Furniture, fixtures and other items were carried from the smoking buildings. One witness saw a piano being taken away in a donkey cart. However, in the absence of any police authority, more useful booty was sought from shops that were neither abandoned nor burning. Tobacconists and drapers had their doors kicked in and goods stolen; at McDonnell's Corn Merchants, residents filed out carrying clocks, bicycles and a set of golf clubs. A Blackpool post office was robbed of £250. Emmet Dalton reported, 'starvation has been staring a great many people in the face, and this horrible state of affairs has, to some extent, encouraged looting'.[19]

## FREE STATE ARRIVAL

At about 7.30 p.m. the first National Army troops entered the south side of the city, via Douglas Road. The initial patrol was led by none other than Captain Peadar Conlon, despite his three severed fingertips and buckshot-peppered face. Immediately following was the armoured car 'The Manager', with General Tom Ennis standing up in it like a ship's captain on his bridge. As the soldiers continued down Anglesea Street towards the destroyed City Hall and the burning Union Quay barracks, hundreds of residents emerged from their homes to welcome them.

'Almost straggling', the National Army soldiers slowly filed across the damaged Parnell Bridge. The 'tired, dead tired' troops moved through the thousands who thronged the South Mall. Many civilians cheered, waved handkerchiefs or passed cigarettes to the troops. Some soldiers were 'nearly pulled to bits by the "shawlies" kissing them'. Irish flags were hoisted on many buildings. The troops quickly established outposts in key locations throughout the city. Most soldiers spent the night at the Cork, Bandon and South Coast railway station at Albert Quay. The Victoria Hotel delivered hot drinks and cigarettes to the victors.[20]

The noise of detonating ammunition and exploding grenades could be heard throughout the night. Hundreds stayed to watch the Union Quay blaze, which also consumed an adjoining hardware/marine supplies shop. The flames did not dissipate until after midnight. Abandoned war material proved deadly to a group of young men who found discarded Republican grenades. One blew up, injuring several and killing one youth: 'every bit of his clothing was blown away except one boot'.[21]

'It is reported that the Provisional Government troops received a very warm welcome on entering the town,' recorded British General Macready, 'especially from the young ladies, whose embraces considerably delayed the pursuit of the enemy.' Mick Leahy bitterly reported that the priests at St Augustine's church on Washington Street turned on their porch lights, 'for the soldiers were up on top of the girls there and they had the girls spread-eagled all over the place ... "What about the respectable people," I asked. "They're all gone mad" was the reply.'[22]

The surreal holiday atmosphere continued for hours, as thousands of residents walked about the city in the warm summer twilight. Like pilgrims, they made a circuit past each of the seven separate fires burning around Cork. In doing so, they celebrated the city's deliverance from expected destruction. Flames had not consumed their beloved city centre. People would wake up knowing they still had a job. There had been no Republican last stand to bring death to their doorsteps. Most remarkably of all, the whole despised Civil War seemed to be at an end.

# CHAPTER 9

# AFTERMATH

Situated twenty-one miles west of Cork on the road to Killarney, Macroom Castle was the final destination for hundreds of beaten Republicans. IRA Volunteers came not just from Cork, but also from Kilmallock, Kerry and evacuated garrisons in Fermoy and Mallow. The Republicans were dazed, demoralised and exhausted. Seán O'Fáolain was among the first to arrive:

> We could hear them coming all night in trucks, private cars, by horse and cart, using anything they could commandeer, and when we rose the next morning we surveyed the image of a rout. Some of these men had been fighting non-stop for a week, and as they poured into the grounds of the castle they had fallen asleep where they stopped, on the grass, in motor cars, lying under trucks, anyhow and every how, a sad litter of men.[1]

The next day, Cork No. 1 Brigade officers assembled the men in the castle grounds. Seán Hendrick listened to brief addresses by IRA leaders Tom Crofts and Sandow O'Donovan. The latter 'explained the position and was damning the situation. They could neither be billeted nor fed. They were to make their own way back to Cork and "bomb all around you".' With this disheartening farewell, the Republican field army disbanded. Rifles and ammunition were handed over for safe keeping. Much of the other war material carried to Macroom was either discarded or destroyed. IRA Volunteers here and in Donoughmore had to make the long walk home, to 'slip back into the city like winter foxes'.[2]

## FREE STATE MILITARY SUCCESS, CIVIC ADMINISTRATION, INFRASTRUCTURE AND EXECUTIONS

Following the devastating defeat, numerous Republicans abandoned the fight. 'The lads we brought back had been on duty night and day and they had no rest,' reported Mick Murphy 'whoever wanted to go home we let them go home.' One veteran remembered his comrades 'being fed up with our running out of Cork and they went back to their jobs'. Column leader Pa Murray admitted, 'When we left Cork City I thought the whole thing was finished.'[3]

He was not the only one. The correspondent from *The Times* promised that the only task remaining was 'rounding up scattered groups of marauders'. Liam de Róiste crowed, 'Had they surrendered there would have been more respect for them; but they literally ran hours before the Regulars entered the city.' 'I feel quite safe in saying that the morale of our enemies is practically broken,' reported Emmet Dalton. 'The impression one gets is that many of the people who were fighting were doing so more or less under a delusion.'[4]

Relentlessly, Dalton kept up the pressure. He quickly linked with his forces at Union Hall and Youghal, and then conducted three simultaneous drives to seize the county's population centres. Clonakilty and Bantry were taken on 11 August; the next day it was Kinsale; on 14 August, Charleville and Buttevant were seized; the next day Fermoy, Mitchelstown and Mallow; and on 16 August, Macroom and Millstreet fell. Everywhere, the Republicans withdrew without making a stand, burning local barracks, wrecking the roads behind them and melting away into the hills.

With limited forces, Dalton could only push the IRA out of the towns. He later claimed that simultaneous attacks from General Eoin O'Duffy's forces in north Cork might have enveloped the retreating Republicans and 'the fight would now be over'. Instead, the IRA Volunteers bought themselves enough time to reorganise. Liam Lynch ordered the formation of flying columns of up to thirty-five members and assigned defined operating areas. The Republicans were now poised to launch the kind of guerrilla campaign at which they excelled.[5]

The *Lady Wicklow* returned to Cork with reinforcements and supplies on Friday 11 August. Dalton's forces were further bolstered by new recruits and by pro-Treaty members of the Cork No. 1 Brigade, the latter classified as the Curragh Reserve. Co-ordinated by General Liam Tobin, hundreds flocked to the Free State banner and were armed with extra rifles that had been carried by the *Arvonia*. Dalton had initially landed a total of 850 men across County Cork, but local recruits almost immediately doubled his strength to 1,600. In Cork city alone, 700 British ex-servicemen had secretly been sworn into the National Army before the invasion, and another 500 were ready in Youghal. Initially, Dalton chose to enrol only 200 of these Cork ex-soldiers into his force, and was immediately grateful for their presence. 'I am sorry and I am glad,' he reported to Dublin, 'that they are conspicuous by their better discipline, deportment and efficiency than my other troops.' Still, Dalton did not entirely trust the ex-soldier's loyalty if tested by their former employers. He explained, 'I was also of the opinion that, in arming them, I would be assisting later potential enemies.' As a result, he only accepted the service of a limited number of ex-servicemen.[6]

Dalton was much more critical of the local pro-Treaty IRA Volunteers assimilated into his force, led by Cork's Captain Jeremiah Dennehy. He reported, 'These men are really almost out of control, and only the most drastic action on my part is likely to have the desired effect.' They apparently 'behaved in a disgracingly [*sic*] rude manner towards the citizens while under the influence of drick [*sic*]'. A month later, Dalton stated, 'these men have given me much more trouble than any other unit'.[7]

By this time, Dalton was trying to restore law and order to Cork from his plush Imperial Hotel headquarters. Bishop Cohalan immediately paid him a courtesy visit, as did the city's former ruling elite: 'I have been called upon by hundreds of prominent citizens who, apparently, have nothing better to do than to wait for hours to congratulate me,' reported the bemused Dalton. Liam de Róiste wrote disgustedly of cliques, 'each vying with the other for power and endeavouring to ingratiate themselves with the military victors'. 'The old "toddies",' complained de Róiste, 'were the first to pay Dalton "reverence".'[8]

Dalton issued a proclamation calling on residents 'to organise and administer their own civic affairs', demanding the surrender of all weapons and stolen goods, and appealing for assistance against the IRA. Following his lead, the Cork Chamber of Commerce, Cork Employers' Federation and Cork Farmers' Union formed the Cork Commercial Committee as a provisional municipal government. Essentially, Cork's commercial elite returned to their natural ruling positions, after years of displacement during the Republican reign.

Since the Garda Síochána had not yet arrived in the city, the commercial committee organised an unarmed municipal police force called the 'Cork Civic Patrol'. The force was established with a grant of £1,000 from Cork's leading merchants, who also loaned their male staff to the force. In this way, explained Emmet Dalton, 'the personnel would not be drawn from the ex-soldier class'. While Dalton happily enrolled working-class ex-soldiers into the army, he apparently did not consider them to be suitable for the police, as advertisements called for recruits 'of good education' only. There is no record of how Cork's socialists viewed the new employer-controlled police force, though they finally may have started to doubt the outcome of an Irish class war. The Cork Civic Patrol operated for the next three months.[9]

The Cork Commercial Committee also sought to restore communications in the city. This task was much more challenging because of the Republicans' thorough destruction of Cork's road and railway networks. During the battle for Cork, at least nine bridges were wrecked or damaged by IRA engineers, including important railway structures. Sometimes mines were used to destroy the road surface, but certain bridges were also brought down. By my count, thirty-two bridges around Cork were damaged or wrecked in the week following the Passage landing. These included key arteries such as the Fota railway bridge, Douglas railway viaduct, Coachford Junction Bridge, Leemount Bridge, Annacarty Bridge, Rathcormac railway bridge and the Chetwynd viaduct. For months, the city was cut off from five railway lines: Great Southern and Western; Cork and Macroom; Cork, Blackrock and Passage; Cork, Bandon and South Coast; Cork and Muskerry. Especially regretted was the destruction of the impressive Mallow viaduct, whose collapse on 10 August was heard twenty miles away in the city.

Most major and minor roads were similarly impeded – cut with trenches or blocked by fallen trees. The road wreckage continued throughout the county, isolating virtually every town in Cork. This was by far the most successful and well thought-out aspect of the IRA defence, which illustrates the Republicans' continued adherence to guerrilla tactics. While tactically astute, the transportation destruction was strategically unwise. It added to Cork's economic woes and occurred during harvest time, creating strong animosity among the local population. Even worse, this happened when civilians believed the war was nearly over. If Republicans wanted to understand their growing unpopularity, they needed to look no further than the nearest collapsed bridge.[10]

Destroyed roads hampered the Free State Army's advance into Cork. One National Army soldier serving under Tom Kilcoyne recalled the advance into north Cork as, 'foot slogging all the way crossing fields, ditches, and clearing pockets of resistance'. It took Peadar Conlon (now promoted to commandant) two full days to travel from Cork to Macroom, a distance Republicans covered in two hours. Along the way, Conlon met an elderly woman who mistook his men for returning British soldiers, offered them a kiss and shouted 'Welcome back to you.'[11]

A few weeks later, Conlon found himself in a dispute with his superiors over the fate of a Republican prisoner. General Emmet Dalton had already begun to lobby for the death sentence for captured Republicans: 'It would be better to try them and execute them than shoot them out of hand when I catch them.' On 8 September, Cork No. 1 Brigade's signalling officer, Timothy Kennefick, was captured near Coachford on his way to his mother's funeral. He was taken away in a convoy apparently commanded by Emmet Dalton. During the journey, Free State officers tortured Kennefick, shot him dead and dumped his body on the road. A coroner's inquest, headed by leading Redmondite J. J. Horgan, returned a verdict of murder. The killers were former members of Michael Collins' 'Squad' under Dalton's command. Protesting to Dalton, Peadar Conlon explained that his troops threatened to mutiny if something similar happened again: 'Therefore you will want to tell those officers from Dublin that they will want to stop that kind of work or they will corrupt the army … I oppose that policy in the strongest way.' When reporting the matter to the new commander-in-chief, Richard Mulcahy, Dalton supported the Kennefick killing and denounced Conlon, though he apparently declined to transfer the recent hero of Rochestown. The IRA later added Dalton to a list of Free State officers 'who have ill-treated prisoners, or have acted on the murder gangs'. Though a masterful military commander, Emmet Dalton's hardness should also be considered an essential part of his personality.[12]

## CORK NO. 1 BRIGADE VERSUS THE NATIONAL ARMY

Having disbanded their men, the leaders of Cork No. 1 Brigade met for a conference in their mountain stronghold near Bally-vourney. They had suffered a series of defeats over the previous six weeks and had humiliatingly been chased out of Cork. It was time to face some unpleasant realities about the recent battle.

Cork Republicans and the Free State forces that met in August 1922 were relatively equal. While the National Army troops enjoyed superiority in numbers and firepower (especially artillery), the Cork IRA Volunteers were defending their home ground. The troop quality on both sides was similar. In terms of leadership, Dalton remained in his own class, well beyond the level of Mick Leahy. Yet, elsewhere down the line, the Corkmen matched up well with the Dubliners. Tom Ennis and Sandow O'Donovan were equally sharp operators, who had commanded both large and small bodies of men in combat. Ex-soldier Peadar Conlon could have swapped war stories with former Irish Guardsman Seán Murray. Squad member Tom Kilcoyne had a doppelgänger in Republican street-fighter Mick Murphy, and armoured-car driver Pat McCrea handled his vehicles no better than the resourceful Jim Grey.

The essential difference in the battle was organisation. The Free State Army enjoyed unity of command, built up over the previous four months. Rather than fighting as individuals, experienced National Army officers commanded platoons and companies, and led from the front. British ex-soldiers provided another boost to their ranks, offering steady leadership in rifle squads, and special-ist knowledge in transport and artillery. The National Army had easy access to money, supplies and reinforcements. During the battle, Emmet Dalton deployed his troops properly, kept them in hand, and adjusted and reinforced his advance when needed. His forces fought as a single, integrated unit, and this proved to be their greatest strength.

The Cork IRA had no such structure in place. Built for guerrilla operations, its organisation did not adjust to conventional fighting. Its best fighters and officers were stripped from their units and formed into flying columns that had become seriously degraded by the time of the August landing. The Republicans' method of collective decision-making and ad hoc organisation worked best under a strong local leader such as Seán O'Hegarty. His decisiveness and clarity of purpose was sorely missing in the Battle of Douglas. Cork No. 1 Brigade OC Mick Leahy, 1st Southern Division OC Liam Deasy and IRA chief of staff Liam Lynch failed to marshal their forces, and allowed the initiative to pass to Emmet Dalton. While the Cork Republicans ran a successful guerrilla organisation, they failed as a conventional army in July and August 1922. The leaders of the Cork No. 1 Brigade understood that, if they were to carry on the war, they needed to make a strategic adjustment.

GUERRILLAS AGAIN

At their conference on 20 August 1922, the Cork No. 1 Brigade officers decided to continue the fight. They would follow Liam Lynch's new Operating Order No. 19, setting up flying columns to resume the guerrilla war. Mick Leahy recalled, 'I thought that if you got out into the countryside you could make their rule impossible.' Already, Republicans within the city had started hitting back. Nightly sniper fire targeted National Army patrols and headquarters, and on 18 August a daylight bomb attack at Parliament Bridge wounded several army recruits. Despite initial optimism that the war was over, Cork city soon saw more intense guerrilla fighting than it had experienced against the British.

During their conference, the brigade officers also heard from their special guest, Éamon de Valera. He recognised the futility of further resistance and appealed for a ceasefire. The brigade leaders decided to remain open to a peace settlement along the lines of the army unification agreement of two months earlier. They offered to serve a government committed to 'advancing the Irish nation to its goal of absolute independence', under an Army Council led by Seán O'Hegarty and Florrie O'Donoghue (neutral in this conflict), along with Liam Lynch, Frank Aiken, Seán MacMahon and Emmet Dalton. The latter's inclusion indicated their newfound respect for the Dubliner. Yet the Cork officers seemed unaware of their tumbling value since the heady days of March 1922, when they arrived boldly at the Mansion House in 'The River Lee'. During the previous few weeks they had been defeated convincingly. Every day, the National Army grew larger and strengthened its hold on the country. Continued Republican resistance brought economic misery to civilians, who turned their scorn on the former heroes. Writing fifty years later, one officer, Connie Neenan, considered, 'Even now, it is almost impossible to believe that men who never changed their ideals and who were such splendid and courageous soldiers in the fighting against England were suddenly looked upon as outcasts.' Shaken by the events during the previous weeks, much of the Cork No. 1 Brigade leadership welcomed a return to guerrilla warfare. But other officers felt the political ground shifting beneath their feet, and this would lead to a complete Republican collapse within nine months.[13]

## THE BIG FELLOW'S HOMECOMING

Meanwhile, the triumphant National Army commander-in-chief

Michael Collins arrived in Cork on the night of 20 August. The next morning, Collins and Emmet Dalton visited various Cork banks along the South Mall, to track down lodgements made by Republicans during their occupation. The IRA had collected £100,000 in customs revenue in July, and hidden it in accounts held by sympathisers. Collins began to seize these assets, having asked bank directors to identify suspicious accounts. Collins was notably well versed in finance and figures: with £100,000, the Republicans could fund their resistance for some time. Rather than covert peace talks of which there is no record, the Big Fellow's primary reason for visiting Cork seems to have been to retrieve this missing money.[14]

Following his success with the Cork banks, Collins chose to tour the county with Emmet Dalton on 22 August 1922. IRA 1st Southern Division commander Liam Deasy, 'rated it a fool-hardy act of a brave man'. Collins travelled to Macroom, Bandon, Clonakilty and Rosscarbery, towns that had only been secured by Free State troops a few days previously. The roads were a mess of blown bridges, trenches and fallen trees; hundreds of armed Republicans were moving throughout the area, including some flying columns. Travelling about in a small motorcade was a reckless decision that testified to Collins' hubris. His first stop was Macroom, where he accidentally bumped into neutral IRA leader Florrie O'Donoghue. The commander-in-chief 'was really talking big', according to O'Donoghue. He boasted at the ease with which he drove through the Republican heartland: 'I've been all over this bloody county but no one has said a bloody word to me.'[15]

On the way to Bandon later that morning, Collins' touring car stopped to ask directions at a crossroads pub near Crookstown. At that very moment, many of Collins' most dangerous Republican opponents were sheltering above the pub and in nearby homes. Similarly to the Cork No. 1 Brigade leaders, Cork No. 3 Brigade leaders had gathered to debate continued participation in the Civil War. Their number included some of the most experienced guerrilla fighters in Ireland. The situation was saved by the cool IRA sentry, who hid his rifle in the pub doorway, stepped outside and calmly directed Collins to Bandon. None the wiser, the convoy continued on.

Owing to their thorough destruction of the road network, the Republicans knew they stood along Collins' probable return route to Cork. These IRA Volunteers (including a number of Cork City officers) decided to ambush the convoy on its way back. This would be the officers' first contribution to the new Republican guerrilla offensive. They established a roadblock, deployed a mine, took up firing positions above the road, and waited for Collins during the rest of the afternoon. At about sunset the officers retired to Long's pub for a drink, leaving behind a few men to collect the mine and dismantle the roadblock. It was those remaining Republicans who heard Collins' convoy enter Béal na mBláth. The Irish Civil War in Cork was about to enter a new and more destructive phase.[16]

# ENDNOTES

## INTRODUCTION

1   Mick Leahy, Seán Culhane, Jamie Moynihan, O'Malley notebooks (OMN), University College Dublin Archives (UCD).

2   Bureau of Military History Witness Statements (BMH WS), National Archives: WS 1424, Mick Burke; WS 1480, Dan O'Donovan; WS 1714, Leo Buckley. Dan O'Donovan, Tom Crofts, OMN. *Sunday Express*, 17 May 1959. Robert Langford Draft Pension Statement, U156/3, Cork City and County Archives (CCCA). Connie Neenan Memoir, CCCA. Hansard, House of Commons Debates (HC Deb): 6 April 1922, vol. 152, c.2406; 3 April 1922, vol. 152, cc.1841–4; 5 April 1922, vol. 152, cc.2234–5. Regan, John, *The Irish Counter-Revolution, 1921–1936* (Dublin: Gill & Macmillan, 1999), pp. 114–115. *Irish Independent*, 30 March 1922 and 1, 4 April 1922. *Cork Constitution*, 30 March 1922 and 1, 4 April 1922.

3   Quoted by Neenan, Burke, Crofts and Murphy, see above for citations.

4   The HMS *Heather* was one of the Queenstown Command's Q-Ships.

5   *Sunday Express*, 17 May 1959.

6   Hansard, HC Deb, 3 April 1922, vol. 152, cc.1841–4.

## CHAPTER 1

1   O'Donoghue, Florence, *No Other Law*, pp. 191–192.

2   *The Cork Examiner*, 7–10, 12, 13 December 1921.

3   *Ibid.*, 10, 12 December 1921.

4   *Ibid.*, 7, 9, 10, 12 December 1921.

5   *Cork Constitution*, 31 December 1921, 31 January 1922.

6   *The Cork Examiner*, 8–10, 12 December 1921.

7   1st Southern Division to GHQ, 10 December 1921, P7/A32, Richard Mulcahy papers, UCD.

8   Liam de Róiste diaries, 2 January 1922, CCCA.

9   *Cork Constitution*, 3 January 1922.

10 De Róiste diaries, 2, 5, 22, 31 January 1922, 2 February 1922, CCCA; *Cork Constitution*, 3 January 1922.

11 *The Times* (London), 28 December 1921, 6, 7 January 1922; Mick Murphy, OMN.

12 *The Cork Examiner*, 3 January 1922.

13 *Cork Constitution*, 15, 31 December 1921, 2, 3 January 1922.

14 *The Cork Examiner*, 9 January 1922.

15 *Ibid.*, 10 January 1922.

16 Florence O'Donoghue, notes of 31 August 1929 on The American Commission on Conditions in Ireland, Pamphlet, P48c/267, papers of Terence MacSwiney's biographers, UCD.

17 *Cork Constitution*, 20 February 1921.

18 For example, Seán O'Sullivan, Pat Higgins, Pat Brady, Michael O'Cuill, Diarmuid Fawsitt, Harry Lorton, Maurice O'Connor and Michael Mehigan.

19 For details on the Cumann na mBan split, see the Cumann na mBan Cork District Council meeting minutes, 1918–21, 2007-38-21, and 1921–2, 2007-38-23, Cork Public Museum; and BMH WS 1576, Peg Duggan and WS 1561, Margaret Lucy.

20 De Róiste diaries, 16, 23 February 1922.

21 McCarthy, Kieran, *Republican Cobh and the East Cork Volunteers since 1913*, pp. 141–145; Mick Leahy, Tom Crofts, Stan Barry O'Malley, OMN; Jeremiah Denney to chief of staff, 3 June 1922, P7B/26, Mulcahy papers; chief of staff to commander-in-chief, 7 June 1922, P7B/26, Mulcahy papers.

22 *Cork Constitution*, 20 February 1922; *Irish Independent*, 20 February 1922.

23 *Irish Independent*, 13, 14 March 1922; *The Irish Times*, 14 March 1922; *Cork Constitution*, 14 March 1922.

24 Cork Corporation meeting minutes, 25 February, 4, 10, 24 March, 7 April 1922, CP/CO/M14, CCCA.

25 De Róiste diaries, 14, 15 March 1922, CCCA; *Irish Independent*, 20 March 1922; *Cork Constitution*, 20 March 1922.

**CHAPTER 2**

1 *Cork Constitution*, 14, 19, 20, 21, 25, 28, 30 January 1922, 2, 27 February 1922, 14 April 1922; *Irish Independent*, 15 April 1922.

2   *Cork Constitution*, 14, 30, 31 January 1922, 1–4, 6, 8–11, 13, 14 February 1922; *The Freeman's Journal*, 1–3, 6–11 February 1922; *Southern Star*, 4 February 1922.

3   *Cork Constitution*, 9, 11 February 1922; *The Freeman's Journal*, 11 February 1922.

4   *Cork Constitution*, 12, 15–17, 19 May 1922.

5   *Ibid.*, 27 January 1922; *The Freeman's Journal*, 8–10 February 1922.

6   *Cork Constitution*, 12, 15–17, 19 May 1922.

7   *Ibid.*, 25 March 1922, 6 April 1922; Bradley, Dan, *Farm Labourers: Irish Struggle 1900–1976*, p. 63.

8   *Cork Constitution*, 3 June 1922; *The Cork Examiner*, 3 June 1922.

9   *Cork Constitution*, 6 April, 19, 24 May 1922; *The Cork Examiner*, 17, 19 May 1922; *Irish Independent*, 31 May 1922.

10  *Cork Constitution*, 24, 25 March, 6, 8 April, 2, 3, 5, 9 June 1922.

11  *The Cork Examiner*, 29 May 1922, 30 June 1922; *Cork Constitution*, 2, 3 June 1922.

12  *The Cork Examiner*, 19 May, 8 June 1922.

13  *The Irish Times*, 9 May 1922.

14  *Cork Constitution*, 5 April 1922.

15  For two different interpretations see Hart, Peter, *The I.R.A. & Its Enemies: Violence and Community in Cork 1916–1923*, pp. 277–292; and Ryan, Meda, *Tom Barry: IRA Freedom Fighter*, pp. 156–170. In a recent article, Jasper Ungoed-Thomas argues that the killings were political rather than sectarian; see 'IRA Sectarianism in Skibbereen?', *Skibbereen and District Historical Society Journal*, vol. 6, 2010.

16  *Cork Constitution*, 29 April 1922, 1 May 1922; *The Cork Examiner*, 1, 5, 6, 8, 9, 11, 13, 17, 18 May 1922; *Southern Star*, 24 June 1922; *Irish Independent*, 3, 4, 8, 10, 12 May 1922.

17  *Cork Constitution*, 1 May 1922; *The Cork Examiner*, 5, 6 May 1922.

18  *The Cork Examiner*, 12, 21, 23 June 1922, 8 July 1922.

19  Murphy, Gerard, *The Year of Disappearances: Political Killings in Cork 1920–1921* (Dublin: Gill & Macmillan, 2010).

20  See my review in *History Ireland*, vol. 19, January/February 2011.

21  Seán Culhane, Charlie Brown OMN; BMH WS 1521, Michael Walsh; British government cabinet meeting, 20 June 1922, CAB/24/137, Kew National Archives, UK (Kew); *Irish Independent*, 1 May 1922; *Cork Constitution*, 1 May 1922; *The Irish Times*, 1 May

1922, 12 July 1922; Brady, A. J. S., *The Briar of Life*, pp. 194–196.

22 Report of the general officer commander-in-chief on the Situation in Ireland for week ended 13 May 1922 (Report on the Situation in Ireland), CAB/24/136, Kew; Report on the Situation in Ireland for week ended 20 June 1922, CAB/24/137, Kew; Hansard, HC Deb, 8, 10, 11, 30, 31 May, 20, 26 June, 4, 11, 19, 25, 27 July 1922; Hamilton, Nigel, *Monty: The Making of a General, 1887–1942*, pp. 162–163; McMahon, Paul, *British Spies and Irish Rebels, British Intelligence and Ireland, 1916–1945*, p. 67; *The Irish Times*, 25 May 1922; Record of Activities of 6th Battalion, Cork No. 1 Brigade, Florrie O'Donoghue papers, MS 31,339, NLI.

23 *Irish Independent*, 12–14 December 1923.

24 *The Cork Examiner*, 25 April 1922; *The Freeman's Journal*, 25 April 1922; *Irish Independent*, 25 April 1922.

25 *The Freeman's Journal*, 27 April 1922.

26 Dáil Éireann historical debates, vol. 2, 3 May 1922.

27 Hopkinson, Michael, *Green Against Green*, pp. 100–104; O'Donoghue, *No Other Law*, pp. 240–244.

28 Tom Crofts, OMN; de Róiste diaries, 25 April, 1, 19 May 1922, CCCA.

29 O'Donoghue, *No Other Law*, pp. 333–334; Seán Murray, OMN.

30 *The Freeman's Journal*, 18, 19 May 1922; *Irish Independent*, 19 May 1922; *Cork Constitution*, 19 May 1922; *The Cork Examiner*, 19 May 1922.

31 *Cork Constitution* 7, 12 June 1922; *The Cork Examiner* 12, 14, 15 June 1922; *The Irish Times*, 12, 15 June 1922; *The Freeman's Journal*, 12, 15 June 1922; Liam de Róiste diaries, 20, 29 May, 3, 6, 7, 10, 11, 14, 15 June 1922, CCCA.

32 *The Irish Times*, 12 June 1922.

33 *The Freeman's Journal*, 16 June 1922; *The Irish Times*, 17, 19 June 1922; *The Cork Examiner*, 17, 19 June 1922; de Róiste diaries, 17 June 1922, CCCA.

34 *Voice of Labour*, 24 June 1922.

35 Kissane, Bill, *The Politics of the Irish Civil War*, pp. 72.

36 Hart, Peter, *The I.R.A. at War 1916–1923*, pp. 194–222. This remains a contested issue, with some historians attributing the assassination order to Michael Collins. For opposing views, see Hopkinson, *Green*

*Against Green*, pp. 112–114; Regan, *The Irish Counter-Revolution*, pp. 71–73.

37  Kissane, *The Politics of the Irish Civil War*, p. 74; Hopkinson, *Green Against Green*, pp. 112–122.

**CHAPTER 3**

1  Hopkinson, *Green Against Green*, pp. 146–148; Liam Deasy, *Brother Against Brother*, pp. 51–54.

2  *Southern Star*, 19 August 1922; *The New York Times*, 3 July 1922; *Irish Independent*, 3 July 1922; De Róiste diaries, 1, 3, 4 July 1922, CCCA.

3  Summary of Accounts, B Company, 13 July to 10 August 1922, PR6-28A, Seamus Fitzgerald papers, CCCA; Cork No. 4 Brigade quartermaster to 1st Sth. Div. quartermaster, 26 July 1922, Captured Documents (CD), Lot 3–4, Military Archives (MA).

4  De Róiste diaries, 6 July 1922, CCCA.

5  For example, Con O'Connell, Thomas Long, Con Regan and P. Fitzgerald. See also the cases of John Chambers, Breen Matthews, Tim O'Callaghan and William Gough, *The Cork Examiner*, 18 July 1922.

6  *The Cork Examiner*, 7, 27 July 1922.

7  *Cork Constitution*, 7 July 1922.

8  De Róiste diaries, 5 July 1922, CCCA.

9  *Ibid.*, 7 July 1922, CCCA.

10  *The Cork Examiner*, 7 July 1922; *Cork Constitution*, 7 July 1922.

11  *The Cork Examiner*, 6 July 1922.

12  *Ibid.*; de Róiste diaries, 3 July 1922, CCCA.

13  *The Cork Examiner*, 3 July 1922.

14  *Ibid.*, 3, 21 July, 29 September 1922; *Irish Independent*, 24 July 1922; de Róiste diaries, 16 July 1922, CCCA; George Hendrick, OMN; Dolan, Anne and O'Malley, Cormac, *'No Surrender Here!'*, pp. 47, 51.

15  De Róiste diaries, 6 July 1922, CCCA.

16  *Irish Independent*, 10 August 1922.

17  *Ibid.*, 12 August 1922.

18  Ó Tuama, Aodh, 'Cork Republican Silver', *Irish Arts Review*, vol. 1, no. 2 (Summer 1984), pp. 52–53.

19  Linge, John, 'The Royal Navy and the Irish Civil War,' *Irish Historical Studies*, vol. 31, no. 121, May 1998, p. 68.

20 *The Irish Times*, 14 June 1922; *The Cork Examiner*, 7 August 1922.

21 *The Irish Times*, 18, 26, 28 July 1922; *Irish Independent*, 27 July 1922; Cork No. 1 Brigade adjutant to OC 1st Sth. Div., 8 July 1922, CD, Lot 3–1, MA.

22 De Róiste diaries, 15 July 1922, CCCA.

23 OC 1st Sth. Div. to adjutant-general, GHQ, 17 July 1922, CD, Lot 3–1, MA; *The Irish Times*, 7 August 1922; *Irish Independent*, 27 July 1922; *The Freeman's Journal*, 11 August 1922; *Southern Star*, 19 August 1922; Captain Somerville to Admiralty, 31 July 1922, CO 739/3, Kew (all Somerville references, copy courtesy of Tom Mahon, Hawaii).

24 1st Sth. Div. OC to adjutant Cork No. 1 Brigade, 10 July 1922; 1st Sth. Div. OC to adjutant-general, GHQ, 17 July 1922; 1st Sth. Div. OC to 1st Sth. Div. OC Civil Affairs, 18 July 1922; 1st Sth. Div. OC to OC Kerry No. 1 Brigade and OC Kerry No. 2 Brigade, 18 July 1922, CD Lot 3–1, MA.

25 1st Sth. Div. adjutant to OC 1st Sth. Div., 13 September 1922; brigade quartermaster to 1st Sth. Div. adjutant, 6 October 1922; 1st Sth. Div. quartermaster to OC 1st Sth. Div., 19 October 1922, CD Lot 3–4, MA.

26 Cork Corporation Law and Finance Committee meeting minutes (Corporation Law and Finance), 25 August 1922, 27 September 1922, CP/C/CM/LF/A, CCCA; OC 1st Sth. Div. to adjutant-general GHQ, 17 July 1922, CD Lot 3–1, MA.

27 *The Irish Times*, 7 August 1922; *Irish Independent*, 9 August 1922.

28 Captain Somerville to Admiralty, 31 July 1922, CO 739/3, Kew.

29 *The Irish Times*, 7 August 1922.

30 *Southern Star*, 19 August 1922; *The Freeman's Journal*, 7 August 1922; *The Irish Times*, 7 August 1922; *Irish Independent*, 9 August 1922; *Nenagh Guardian*, 12 August 1922; Captain Somerville to Admiralty, 14 July 1922, CO 739/3, Kew.

31 Cork Harbour Commissioners meeting minutes (Harbour Commissioners), 6 September 1922, vol. 54, Port of Cork Archives.

32 *The Irish Times*, 28 July, 7 August 1922; *Irish Independent*, 9 August 1922; Nyhan, Miriam, *'Are You Still Below?': The Ford Marina Plant, Cork, 1917–1984*, p. 44.

33 De Róiste diaries, 23, 26, 30 July, 3 August 1922, CCCA; 'Report

on the Situation in Cork by M. [Murt] O'Connell', 19 July 1922, P17B/41, Mulcahy papers, UCD (O'Connell Report, Mulcahy papers, UCD); *Southern Star*, 19 August 1922; Connie Neenan memoir, CCCA.

34 *Irish Independent*, 10 August 1922.

35 Cork No. 1 Brigade adjutant to OC 9th Battalion, 22 July 1922, CD, Lot 107, MA; Seán Culhane, Mick Murphy, Jamie Moynihan, OMN.

36 *The Cork Examiner*, 17, 26 July 1922.

37 De Róiste diaries, 19, 27 July 1922, CCCA; *The Cork Examiner*, 24 July, 22 August 1922; *The Irish Times*, 10, 15 August 1922; National Troop Prisoner of War Transfers, 19, 22, 26 July 1922, CP-P-02-01-12, MA.

38 Cork No. 1 Brigade adjutant to 1st Sth. Div. adjutant, 26 July 1922, MA.

39 *The Cork Examiner*, 31 July 1922.

40 Connie Neenan memoir, CCCA.

41 Seán Hendrick, OMN.

42 *The Cork Examiner*, 25 September 1922.

43 *The Cork Examiner*, 25–29 July, 1, 8 August 1922.

44 *Irish Independent*, 27 July, 2, 4, 10 August 1922; *The Irish Times*, 26, 29 July, 3, 4, 7 August 1922.

45 *Irish Independent*, 2 August 1922; *The Irish Times*, 3 August 1922.

46 *The Cork Examiner*, 2 August 1922; *The Irish Times*, 7 August 1922; *Nenagh Guardian*, 12 August 1922; Seán Hendrick, OMN; Harbour Commissioners, 19 July 1922, vol. 54, Port of Cork Archives.

47 *The Cork Examiner*, 7 July 1922; *Irish Independent*, 2 August 1922. Cork No. 1 Brigade adjutant to OC 1st Sth. Div., 8 July 1922; GS&WR District Superintendent William Thompson to Commandant General Liam Deasy, 11 July 1922; OC 1st Sth. Div. to adjutant general GHQ, 17 July 1922, CD, Lot 3–1, MA.

48 *The Irish Times*, 26 July 1922; *Irish Independent*, 27 July 1922; *The Cork Examiner*, 27 July 1922.

49 *The Cork Examiner*, 27 July, 4 August 1922.

50 *Cork Constitution*, 13 July 1922.

51 O'Connell Report, Mulcahy papers, UCD.

52 *Irish Independent*, 2 August 1922.

53  *The Cork Examiner*, 14, 21 July 1922.

54  *Ibid.*, 11, 24 July, 5 August 1922.

55  *Irish Independent*, 19 July, 2 August 1922; *The New York Times*, 25 July 1922; *The Freeman's Journal*, 7 August 1922.

56  *The Cork Examiner*, 19 July 1922.

57  *Cork Constitution*, 13, 14, 17 July 1922; *The Cork Examiner*, 15, 18 July 1922.

58  *The Cork Examiner*, 18 July 1922.

59  *The Cork Examiner*, 22, 24, 26 July 1922; *Irish Independent*, 25 July 1922; *The Irish Times*, 27 July 1922.

60  *The Cork Examiner*, 2 August 1922.

61  *Ibid.*, 7 August 1922; *The Irish Times*, 7 August 1922.

62  *Voice of Labour*, 5 August 1922. For more details, see also the *Voice of Labour* 22, 29 July 1922; *The Freeman's Journal*, 8 August 1922.

63  *The Cork Examiner*, 7 August 1922.

**CHAPTER 4**

1  Tom Crofts, Patrick O'Sullivan, OMN.

2  Patrick O'Sullivan, OMN.

3  Moss Twomey, OMN.

4  Tom Crofts, OMN.

5  Mick O'Sullivan, OMN. O'Sullivan was quoting the former British officer David Robinson, then serving with the IRA west of Macroom.

6  Quartermaster General Department Report, 15 July 1922, P7B/3, Mulcahy papers, UCD.

7  *Southern Star*, 26 August 1922.

8  Mick Leahy, OMN.

9  Dolan and O'Malley, *'No Surrender Here!'*, p. 45.

10  Ó Ruairc, Pádraig Óg, *The Battle for Limerick city*.

11  Jamie Moynihan, Stan Barry, Mick Leahy, OMN.

12  Dolan and O'Malley, *'No Surrender Here!'*, pp. 51, 55–56, 68–69.

13  Seán Culhane, Mick Leahy, Mick Murphy, OMN.

14  Connie Neenan memoir, CCCA.

15  Dolan and O'Malley, *'No Surrender Here!'*, p. 55; Mick Leahy, Pat Sullivan, 'Sandow' O'Donovan, OMN; Tom Hales to OC 1st Sth. Div., 26 July 1922, CD, Lot 3, MA; Paddy Cahill to OC Kerry No. 1 Brigade, 15 July 1922, CD, Lot 4, MA; Tom Hales to OC 1st Sth.

Div., 13 July 1922, CD, Lot 4, MA.

16  Dolan and O'Malley, *'No Surrender Here!'*, pp. 62, 75–76, 80–83, 86–87.

17  *Ibid.*, pp. 51, 55, 68–69, 72, 82–84.

18  Hopkinson, *Green Against Green*, p. 145.

19  Eamon Enright, OMN. Potential landing spots included Fenit, Tarbert, Dingle (town), Ardmore, Dungarvan, Castletownbere, Bantry, Glengarriff, Baltimore, Union Hall, Kinsale, Cork Harbour, Ballycotton and Youghal.

20  *The Freeman's Journal*, 1, 15 August 1922; *Irish Independent*, 9 August 1922; *The Irish Times*, 10 August 1922; *The Cork Examiner*, 26 August 1922; Gibbs Ross, OC Cork No. 5 Brigade, to OC 1st Sth. Div., 1 August 1922, CD Lot 3–4, MA; OC 1st Sth. Div. to GHQ Director of Engineering, 9 July 1922, CD Lot 3–3, MA.

21  Linge, 'The Royal Navy and the Irish Civil War', p. 66. These requests were made at the end of July and early August before the Passage landing.

22  Linge, 'The Royal Navy and the Irish Civil War', pp. 63–64, 66, 67; *The Cork Examiner*, 1 August 1922.

23  Captain Somerville to Admiralty, 5 July 1922, CO 739/3, Kew.

24  Statements of Edward Butler, 9, 21 September 1942, G. Grassley, 25 September 1942, Seamus Fitzgerald papers, PR6-38A, CCCA; *The Irish Times*, 14 August 1922; *Southern Star*, 19 August 1922; Captain Somerville to Admiralty, 5 July 1922, CO 739/3, Kew.

25  *The Irish Times*, 28 July, 10 August 1922; *The Cork Examiner*, 20 July, 3, 22, 31 August 1922; *Irish Independent*, 21 July, 10 August 1922; *The Freeman's Journal*, 1, 10 August 1922; Cork Harbour Commission Dredge and Water Works Committee meeting minutes (Dredge and Water Works), 10, 17, 24 July 1922, vol. 17, Port of Cork Archives.

26  Cha and Miah were two fictional Cork figures played by Frank Duggan and Michael Twomey, who dressed in long coats and flat caps, sat on a park bench and gave their own unique take on the politics of the day.

27  *The Cork Examiner*, 3 August 1922; *Irish Independent*, 10 August 1922; Harbour Commissioners meeting minutes, 2 August 1922, vol. 54, Port of Cork Archives.

28  Harbour Commissioners meeting minutes, 16 August 1922 (see 15

August report of the Acting Harbour Master), 30 August 1922, Port of Cork Archives; *The Irish Times*, 10 August 1922; *The Cork Examiner*, 12 September 1922; O'Connell Report, Mulcahy papers, UCD. IRA commander Mick Burke seems to have deliberately spread rumours of such mines. See Neeson, Eoin, *The Civil War in Ireland*, p. 252.

29 Colman O'Mahony has good coverage of War of Independence activity in the area, in *The Maritime Gateway to Cork, A History of the Outports of Passage and Monkstown, 1754–1942*.

30 BMH WS 1505, Ed Sisk; BMH WS 1506, Henry O'Mahoney. 9th Battalion quartermaster company arms returns, 25 January 1922; headquarters strength, 9th Battalion, *circa* late July 1922; undated battalion strength return, *circa* July 1922; brigade adjutant to all battalion OCs, 10 July 1922; brigade adjutant to OC 9th Battalion, 12 July 1922; brigade adjutant to OC 9th Battalion, 21 July 1922; brigade intelligence officer to OC 9th Battalion, 31 July 1922, CD, Lot 107, MA. Additional information courtesy of Colman O'Mahony.

31 Tom Crofts, Mick Leahy, OMN.

32 OC 9th Battalion to brigade adjutant, 17 July 1922, CD, Lot 107, MA; adjutant, 9th Battalion to brigade adjutant (attached to previous).

33 Captain Somerville to Admiralty, 14 July 1922, CO 739/3, Kew; O'Connell Report, Mulcahy papers, UCD.

**CHAPTER 5**

1 Brunicardi, Lt Cdr Daire, 'The Ships of the Army 1922', *An Cosantóir*, vol. 49, no. 3, March 1989, p. 32; McIvor, Aidan, *A History of the Irish Naval Service*, pp. 43–44, 46; Hopkinson, *Green Against Green*, p. 163; Ó Confhaola, Padhraic, 'The Naval Forces of the Irish State, 1922–1977', unpublished PhD dissertation, NUI Maynooth, 2009.

2 See Doyle, Tom, *The Summer Campaign in Kerry*; Harrington, Niall, *Kerry Landing*; Dwyer, T. Ryle, *Tans, Terror and Trouble: Kerry's Real Fighting Story, 1913–1923*.

3 Harrington, *Kerry Landing*, pp. 70–71.

4 J. J. Walsh Report, 13 July 1922, P7B/106, Mulcahy papers, UCD.

5 O'Connell Report, Mulcahy papers, UCD; 'Memo from C', 12 July 1922, P7B/106 may also have emanated from O'Connell.

6 Captain Somerville to Admiralty, 14 July 1922, CO 739/3, Kew; General Emmet Dalton to commander-in-chief, 13 September 1922,

CW-OPS-04-01, MA; commander-in-chief to director of intelligence, 27 July 1922, P7B/4, Mulcahy papers, UCD.

7   Ryan, Meda, *The Day Michael Collins Was Shot*, pp. 176–177.

8   Dalton to commander-in-chief, 12 August 1922, P7B/20, Mulcahy papers, UCD; Dalton to commander-in-chief, 13 September 1922, CW-OPS-04-01, MA.

9   Senator James Phelan, notes from an interview with Michael Collins in Liam Cosgrave's office, 31 July 1922, Phelan papers, Box 28, Bancroft Library, University of California, Berkeley.

10  *The Irish People*, 13 August 1922.

11  Economic minister to minister for defence, 9, 11, 12, 15, 16 July 1922, P7B/26, Mulcahy papers, UCD. See also commander-in-chief (Michael Collins) to quartermaster general, 17 July 1922, P7B/3, Mulcahy Papers, regarding advance notice to the British government to prevent Royal Navy interference with seaborne troop movements.

12  Younger, Calton, *Ireland's Civil War*, p. 401.

13  Cottrell, Peter, *The Irish Civil War, 1922–1923*, pp. 60–63; Seán Murray, OMN; *Dictionary of Irish Biography*, vol. 3, pp. 7–9.

14  Ernie O'Malley in *Dublin's Fighting Story*, p. 289.

15  Coleman, Marie, *County Longford and the Irish Revolution, 1910–1923*, p. 187; *The Freeman's Journal*, 5 August 1922.

16  Coleman, *County Longford*, pp. 130, 140, 187, 228; Younger, *Ireland's Civil War*, p. 401.

17  1901 Census Ireland.

18  *Irish Independent*, 3 March 1933.

19  *Sunday Independent*, 6 August 1922.

20  OC Eastern Command to commander-in-chief, 7 August 1922, P7B/16, Mulcahy Papers; *The Irish Times*, 10 August 1922; *The Freeman's Journal*, 15 August 1922. Correspondents represented *The Irish Times* and *The Freeman's Journal*. See also the British Cabinet Report on the Situation in Ireland for the week ending 5 August 1922, CAB/24/138, Kew.

21  See the Hogan Wilson Collection at the National Photographic Archive, Dublin.

22  Captain Somerville to Admiralty, 9 August 1922, CO 739/3, Kew; McCarthy, *Republican Cobh*, p. 196; Younger, *Ireland's Civil War*, pp. 400–401.

23 *The Irish Times*, 10 August 1922; *The Cork Examiner*, 12 September 1922; O'Connell Report, Mulcahy papers, UCD.

24 Younger, *Ireland's Civil War*, pp. 400–401; Captain Somerville to Admiralty, 9 August 1922, CO 739/3, Kew; Neeson, Geraldine, *In My Mind's Eye: The Cork I Knew and Loved*, p. 253.

25 *The Irish Times*, 15 August 1922; *The Freeman's Journal*, 15 August 1922; Dr James Lynch, 'The Battle of Douglas', typescript, Cork City Library.

26 Information received by author from Colman O'Mahony.

27 *The Freeman's Journal*, 10 August 1922; *The Irish Times*, 10 August 1922; *The Times* (London), 10 August 1922; *Southern Star*, 12, 19 August 1922; *Munster Express*, 12 August 1922; Captain Somerville to Admiralty, 9 August 1922.


**CHAPTER 6**

1 Lynch, 'The Battle of Douglas'.

2 *The Irish Times*, 10 August 1922; *The Freeman's Journal*, 12, 15, 16 August 1922. Aerial Reconnaissance Report, 10 August 1922, P7B/10; Wireless Message, Liam [Tobin] to commander-in-chief, 10 August 1922, P7B/20, Mulcahy papers, UCD.

3 Harbour Commission, 16 August 1922, vol. 54, Port of Cork Archives; *The Cork Examiner*, 12 August 1922.

4 Seán Murray, OMN; *The Freeman's Journal*, 11, 15 August 1922; *The Irish Times*, 15 August 1922.

5 'Sandow' O'Donovan, OMN; White and Harvey, *A History of Victoria/Collins Barracks*, p. 105; Lynch, 'The Battle of Douglas'; *Munster Express*, 12 August 1922.

6 *The Freeman's Journal*, 11, 15 August 1922. The soldier was variously described as Private James Garvin, Private J. S. Cunningham of Mullingar, and Private J. S. Gannaghan, Mill Road, Dublin.

7 Murray, OMN; Lynch, 'The Battle of Douglas'.

8 Lynch, 'The Battle of Douglas'.

9 *The Cork Examiner*, 12 August 1922.

10 Lynch, 'The Battle of Douglas'. See also the George Gunn interview (audiotape, author's possession, courtesy Pat Gunn); Hopkinson, *Green Against Green*, p. 164; Dolan and O'Malley, *'No Surrender Here!'*, p. 91.

11 Hopkinson, *Green Against Green*, p. 164; *Munster Express*, 12 August 1922; 'Sandow' O'Donovan, Mick Murphy, Seán Culhane, Seán Murray, Frank O'Malley, OMN.

12 *The Irish Times*, 10 August 1922; *Irish Independent*, 12 August 1922; *The Cork Examiner*, 14, 19, 31 August, 16 October 1922; *Southern Star*, 19 August 1922; Captain Somerville to Admiralty, 13 August 1922, CO 739/3, Kew.

13 *The Freeman's Journal*, 12 August 1922.

14 *The Cork Examiner*, 12 August 1922; *The Freeman's Journal*, 12 August 1922; *Irish Independent*, 12 August 1922.

15 *The Times* (London), 11 August 1922; *The New York Times*, 12–13 August 1922; *Nenagh Guardian*, 12 August 1922; *Munster Express*, 12, 19 August 1922; O'Connor, Frank, *An Only Child*, p. 228.

16 *Irish Independent*, 12 August 1922; *The Freeman's Journal*, 12 August 1922; *The Cork Examiner*, 29 September 1922.

17 *The Cork Examiner*, 19 August 1922; additional information courtesy of Cork Fire Brigade historian, Pat Poland.

18 *The Freeman's Journal*, 12 August 1922.

19 *The New York Times*, 11, 12 August 1922; White and Harvey, *A History of Victoria/Collins Barracks*, pp. 105–106; *The Freeman's Journal*, 12 August 1922; *The Irish Times*, 15 August 1922.

**CHAPTER 7**

1 *The Freeman's Journal*, 10 August 1922; *The Irish Times*, 10 August 1922.

2 Cork Harbour Commission, Dredge and Water Works Committee meeting minutes, 8 August 1922 (subsequently Dredge and Water Works), Port of Cork Archives.

3 Linge, 'The Royal Navy and the Irish Civil War', pp. 63–64; Captain Somerville to Admiralty, 9 August 1922, CO 739/3, Kew; Harbour Commissioners, 30 August 1922, vol. 54, Port of Cork Archives; Dredge and Water Works, 4 September 1922, Port of Cork Archives; *The Cork Examiner*, 31 August, 15 September 1922. The IRA assassinated Somerville's brother, Admiral Henry Somerville, in 1936 for signing recommendation letters for local men entering the Royal Navy. His killing was unpopular and controversial in Cork.

4 Harbour Commissioners, 16, 30 August 1922, vol. 54, Port of Cork

Archives; *The Times* (London), 12 August 1922.

5   O'Connor, Emmet, 'Communists, Russia, and the IRA, 1920–1923', vol. 46, no. 1, *The Historical Journal*, 2003, p. 120; *The New York Times*, 12 August 1922; *The Irish Times*, 14 August 1922.

6   *The Irish Times*, 14 August 1922; *The Freeman's Journal*, 15 August 1922; *The Cork Examiner*, 16 October 1922. Statement of Edward Butter, 9 September 1942; Seamus Fitzgerald Pension Statement, 24 July 1942, PR6-38A, CCCA; Mick Leahy, OMN.

7   *Irish Independent*, 12 August 1922; *The Irish Times*, 14 August 1922; *The Cork Examiner*, 12 August 1922; Lynch, 'The Battle of Douglas'; Neeson, *The Civil War in Ireland*, p. 257.

8   Lynch, 'The Battle of Douglas'.

9   *Ibid.*

10   *Ibid.*; Neeson, *The Civil War in Ireland*, p. 256; Younger, *Ireland's Civil War*, p. 406. Younger does not mention the five men killed. I am assuming this is the same action described in the *The Cork Examiner*, 16 October 1922.

11   Lynch, 'The Battle of Douglas'.

12   *Ibid.*

13   *The Cork Examiner*, 12 August 1922.

14   Lynch, 'The Battle of Douglas'; Neeson, *The Civil War in Ireland*, p. 256; White and Harvey, *A History of Victoria/Collins Barracks, Cork*, p. 258; Younger, *Ireland's Civil War*, pp. 406–407.

15   *Irish Independent*, 8 October 1922; *Southern Star*, 16 August 1924; *Kerryman*, 4 December 1965; Twohig, Patrick, *Green Tears for Hecuba*; O'Suilleabhain, Micheal, *Where Mountainy Men Have Sown*; 'Padraigh Greene Interview', Ballingeary and Inchigeela Historical Society, *Journal of Ballingeary Cumann Staire*, 2000; and Stephen Coyle's profile in the *Irish Democrat*, 9 August 2006.

16   Neeson, Geraldine, *In My Mind's Eye*, pp. 102–103. Neeson was the mother of writer and historian Eoin Neeson.

17   George Gunn interview.

18   Lynch, 'The Battle of Douglas'; *The Cork Examiner*, 12 August 1922; Younger, *Ireland's Civil War*, p. 407; Frank Busteed, OMN.

19   O'Connor, *An Only Child*, p. 220; Younger, *Ireland's Civil War*, p. 408.

20   Jamie Moynihan, Frank Busteed, 'Sandow' O'Donovan, OMN; George Gunn interview.

21 Dolan and O'Malley, *'No Surrender Here!'*, p. 91.

22 Lynch, 'The Battle of Douglas'; Tom Crofts, OMN.

23 Lynch, 'The Battle of Douglas'.

24 Clarke, Olga Pyne, *She Came of Decent People*, pp. 56–57.

25 *The Irish Times*, 14, 15 August 1922; *Irish Independent*, 12 August 1922.

26 Medical officer Cork No. 1 Brigade to GHQ director of medical services, 1 September 1922, CD, Lot 4; *Irish Independent*, 12 August 1922. These appear to have been Raleigh coupés, the same type of car the Cobh Republicans fitted with machine guns.

27 *The Freeman's Journal*, 11, 15 August 1922.

28 *Ibid.*, 14, 15 August 1922. They were: Patrick Perry, 24, Dublin; William Nevin, 38, Dublin; Gerald MacKenna, 18, Dublin; Thomas Lynch, Dublin Guards; Christopher O'Toole, Dublin Guards; Terence Maguire, Dublin Guards.

29 *The Irish Times*, 12 August 1922; *The New York Times*, 12 August 1922.

30 O'Mahony, *The Maritime Gateway to Cork*, p. 106. His names are: James Moloney, Jerry Hourigan, Christy Olden, Dan McCarthy, Patrick Burns, John P. O'Brien and 'Scottie' McKenzie (Ian McKenzie Kennedy). Wilton historian Richard Henchion lists all those individuals as being buried in St Finbarr's Cemetery, Wilton, Cork, with the exception of Christy Olden. He also adds an eighth name: Patrick Murphy. See Henchion, Richard, *Bishopstown, Wilton, and Glasheen, A Picture of Life in the Three Western Suburbs of Cork from Early Days to Modern Times*, pp. 143–144. Christy Olden was identified as being killed in the battle by IRA veterans Frank Busteed and George Gunn. A Cork IRA death roll (author's possession) names Burns, Hourigan, Moloney, McCarthy, McKenzie and Olden, along with two other possible casualties: Michael Rouse and James Moroney.

31 White and Harvey, *A History of Victoria/Collins Barracks, Cork*, p. 108; *Irish Independent*, 12 August 1922; Corporation Law and Finance, 13 September 1922, CP-C-CM-LF-A, CCCA; *The Cork Examiner*, 29 September 1922.

**CHAPTER 8**

1 Lynch, 'The Battle of Douglas'; *The Cork Examiner*, 12 August 1922; Connie Neenan memoir, CCCA.

2   Connie Neenan memoir, CCCA; Frank Busteed, OMN; George Gunn interview.

3   Lynch to OC 1st Sth. Div., 10 August 1922, CD Lot 3–1, MA; *The Cork Examiner*, 19 August 1922; Cork Corporation meeting minutes, 8 September 1922, CP/CO/M14, CCCA; Mick Murphy, Mick Leahy, OMN.

4   *The Irish Times*, 12 August 1922; White and Harvey, *A History of Victoria/Collins Barracks, Cork*, p. 108; Mick Murphy, OMN.

5   *The Freeman's Journal*, 15 August 1922; *The Irish Times*, 15 August 1922; *The Cork Examiner*, 22 August 1922.

6   Emmet Dalton to commander-in-chief, 13 September 1922, CW-OPS-04-01, MA; Neeson, *The Civil War in Ireland*, p. 258; *The Cork Examiner*, 28 September 1922; *The Irish Times*, 14 August 1922; *The Freeman's Journal*, 14 August 1922.

7   Mick Murphy, Eamon Enright, OMN; O'Connor, *An Only Child*, pp. 227–228; Geraldine Neeson, *In My Mind's Eye*, pp. 103–104.

8   *The Cork Examiner*, 27 September 1922; Corporation Law and Finance, 13 September 1922, CP-C-CM-LF-A, CCCA.

9   George Gunn interview; Records of activities from the 6th Battalion, Cork No. 1 Brigade, Florrie O'Donoghue papers, MS 31,339, National Library of Ireland.

10  George Gunn interview; *The Freeman's Journal*, 14 August 1922.

11  *The Freeman's Journal*, 14 August 1922; *The Irish Times*, 14 August 1922; *The New York Times*, 13 August 1922.

12  *The Irish Times*, 12, 15 August 1922; *The Freeman's Journal*, 14 August 1922; *The New York Times*, 13 August 1922; *The Cork Examiner*, 25 August 1922.

13  White and Harvey, *A History of Victoria/Collins Barracks*, pp. 108–109.

14  *Irish Independent*, 12 August 1922.

15  Aerial Reconnaissance Report, 10 August 1922, P7B/10, Mulcahy Papers, UCD; Liam [General Liam Tobin] to commander-in-chief, 10 August 1922, P7B/20, Mulcahy Papers, UCD.

16  *Irish Independent*, 12 August 1922. For more details, see also: *The Irish Times*, 12 August 1922; *The Cork Examiner*, 28 August 1922.

17  *The Irish Times*, 14 August 1922; *The Freeman's Journal*, 14 August 1922; *Irish Independent*, 12 August 1922; White and Harvey, *A History of Victoria/Collins Barracks*, p. 108.

18  White and Harvey, *A History of Victoria/Collins Barracks*, p. 108. See also *The Freeman's Journal*, 14 August 1922; *Irish Independent*, 12 August 1922.

19  *The Irish Times*, 15 August 1922; *The Cork Examiner*, 23, 26, 27, 28 September 1922; Dalton to commander-in-chief, 12 August 1922, P7B/20, Mulcahy Papers, UCD.

20  White and Harvey, *A History of Victoria/Collins Barracks*, p. 108; *Irish Independent*, 12 August 1922; *The Irish Times*, 14, 15 August 1922; *The Freeman's Journal*, 14 August 1922; *The Cork Examiner*, 19 August 1922.

21  *Irish Independent*, 12 August 1922.

22  Report on the Situation in Ireland, week ended 12 August 1922, CAB/24/138, Kew; Mick Leahy, OMN.

**CHAPTER 9**

1  Seán O'Fáolain, *Vive Moi!*, p. 154.

2  Seán Hendrick, OMN; O'Fáolain, *Vive Moi!*, p. 154.

3  Donal Barrett, Mick Murphy, OMN; Murray quoted in Hopkinson, *Green Against Green*, p. 164; Deasy, *Brother Against Brother*, p. 72.

4  *The Times* (London), 11 August 1922; de Róiste diaries, 20 August 1922, CCCA; Dalton to chief of staff, 12 August 1922.

5  White and Harvey, *A History of Victoria/Collins Barracks*, pp. 258–260.

6  *Ibid.*, p. 258; Dalton to commander-in-chief, 12 August 1922; Dalton to commander-in-chief Richard Mulcahy, 13 September 1922, CW-OPS-04-01.

7  White and Harvey, *A History of Victoria/Collins Barracks*, pp. 258–260.

8  Dalton to commander-in-chief, 12 August 1922; de Róiste diaries, 16, 20 August 1922, CCCA; *The Irish Times* 14, 15 August 1922.

9  Dalton to commander-in-chief, 12 August 1922; Cork Chamber of Commerce and Shipping Annual Report 1922, pp. 9–10, MP 507, Boole Library, University College Cork; *The Cork Examiner*, 14 August, 1, 7, 20 September, 2, 10 October 1922.

10 My count includes: Fota, Parnell, Brian Boru, Parliament, Douglas viaduct, Chetwynd viaduct, Coachford Junction, Leemount, Anna-carty, Rathcormac, Monkstown, Passage, Crosshaven, Ballygroman, Rochestown station, Rochestown Road, Model Farm Road, Crook-stown railway, Coachford Junction, Douglas Bridge (Douglas Mills),

Ballincollig (two railway bridges), Carrigrohane/Leemount, Waterloo/
Blarney, Faggot Hill/Blarney, Iniscarra, Five Mile, Ballinhassig railway,
Ballinhassig roadway, Ringane, Waterfall Road No. 8, Bishopstown
station railway. See *The Irish Times*, 12 August 1922, *Irish Independent*,
12 August 1922; *Southern Star*, 19 August 1922; *The Cork Examiner*,
12, 17, 18, 20, 22 August, 16 October 1922; Jenkins, Stanley, *The Cork,
Blackrock and Passage Railway*, p. 87; Jenkins, Stanley, *The Cork and
Muskerry Light Railway*, p. 29; Creedon, C., *Cork City Railway Stations,
An Illustrated History, 1849–1985*; Cork Chamber of Commerce
Annual Report, 1922, MP 507, University College Cork.

11  *Sunday Independent*, 24 May 1970; *The Cork Examiner*, 19 August
1922.

12  Dolan and O'Malley, *'No Surrender Here!'*, pp. 185, 233, 309; Regan,
*The Irish Counter-Revolution*, 1921–1936, pp. 104–105; Statement
of Mrs Nellie Kennefick, *circa* November 1922, CD, Lot 4, MA;
Dalton to commander-in-chief Richard Mulcahy, 3 September 1922,
CW-OPS-01-02-06, MA; *Poblacht na hÉireann*, 4 October 1922;
Dáil Éireann Parliamentary Debates, vol. I, 18 October 1922, Ques-
tions and vol. I, 1 November, Written Replies, National Archives,
Dublin; Timothy Kennefick Coroner's Inquest Report, courtesy of
Timothy Kennefick Memorial Committee. See also Robert Langford
Papers, U156/13, CCCA.

13  Unification document, *circa* August 1922; chief of staff to all divi-
sions, 19 August 1922, CD, Lot 3–1, MA. Ryan, pp. 61–62; Deasy,
*Brother Against Brother*, p. 76; Connie Neenan memoir, CCCA; Mick
Leahy, OMN; *The Cork Examiner*, 19, 21 August 1922.

14  Ryan, *The Day Michael Collins Was Shot*, pp. 55–57; Younger, *Ireland's
Civil War*, pp. 422–423.

15  Deasy, *Brother Against Brother*, p. 81; *The Cork Examiner*, 14, 15,
17–19, 21, 22 August 1922; Florrie O'Donoghue, OMN.

16  Dan Corkery, OMN; Deasy, *Brother Against Brother*, pp. 77–79;
Ryan, *The Day Michael Collins Was Shot*, pp. 89–105; Hopkinson,
*Green Against Green*, ch. 20. Cork city participants in the ambush
included Tom Crofts, Seán Culhane, Con Lucey, Pete Kearney and
Jim Kearney. The latter three men were both west Cork natives and
UCC students; they served in both Cork city's 'College Company'
and the Cork No. 3 Brigade.

# BIBLIOGRAPHY

**PRIMARY SOURCES**

Bancroft Library, University of California at Berkeley
  Senator James Phelan papers
Kew National Archives, London
  Cabinet papers (CAB)
  Colonial Office (CO)
  War Office (WO)
Military Archives, Cathal Brugha Barracks, Dublin
  Civil War Collection
        Operations (CW-OPS)
        Captured Documents (CD)
National Archives, Dublin
  Bureau of Military History Witness Statements (BMH WS)
  Dáil Éireann Department of Local Government
National Library of Ireland (NLI)
  Florence O'Donoghue papers
University College Dublin Archives (UCD)
  Richard Mulcahy papers
  Papers of Terence MacSwiney's biographers
  Ernie O'Malley notebooks (OMN)
      P17B/95: Stan Barry, Florrie O'Donoghue, Dan 'Sandow'
        O'Donovan
      P17B/103: Eamon Enright
      P17B/108: Tadg O'Sullivan, Tom Crofts, Seán Culhane, Mick
        Leahy, Mick O'Sullivan
      P17B/111: Dan Corkery, Donal Barrett, Seán Hendrick, Seamus
        Fitzgerald, Ray Kennedy, Patrick O'Sullivan
      P17B/112: Mick Murphy, Charlie Browne, Seán Murray, Jamie
        Moynihan, Frank Busteed

Port of Cork
    Cork Harbour Commission meeting minutes
    Cork Harbour Commission, Law and Finance Committee meeting
       minutes
    Cork Harbour Commission, Dredge and Water Works Committee
       meeting minutes
Cork City and County Archives (CCCA)
    Cork Corporation meeting minutes
    Cork Corporation Law & Finance Committee meeting minutes
    Connie Neenan memoir
    Liam de Róiste diaries
       U271A-42: I, 1 January 1922–19 February 1922
       U271A-43: 22 February 1922–30 April 1922
       U271A-44: 1 May 1922–29 June 1922
       U271A-45: 29 June 1922–3 August 1922
       U271A-46: 16 August 1922–31 August 1922
    Barry Egan papers
    Seamus Fitzgerald papers
Cork City Library Local Studies Department
    Dr James Lynch, typescript, 'The Battle of Douglas'
    Guys Directory
Boole Library, University College Cork
    British in Ireland Series (Microfilm) – Colonial Office, CO 904
    Munster Printing (MP) – Cork Chamber of Commerce and Shipping
    Annual Report


**PRIVATE COLLECTIONS**

George Gunn Interview (audio tape), courtesy Pat Gunn
Timothy Kennefick Coroner's Inquest copy, courtesy of Captain Timothy
    Kennefick Memorial Committee
Cork IRA Roll of Honour, author's possession


**OFFICIAL PUBLICATIONS**

Dáil Éireann Parliamentary Debates
Hansard: House of Commons Debates

## NEWSPAPERS

*Cork Constitution*
*Cork Examiner, The*
*Éire Óg*
*Freeman's Journal, The*
*Free State, The*
*Irish Independent*
*Irish People*
*Irish Times, The*
*Munster Express*
*Nenagh Guardian*
*New Ireland*
*New York Times, The*
*Sunday Independent*
*Southern Star*
*Times, The* (London)
*Voice of Labour*

## SECONDARY WORKS

Borgonovo, John (ed.), *Florence and Josephine O'Donoghue's War of Independence, A Destiny that Shapes Our Ends* (Dublin: Irish Academic Press, 2006)

Bradley, Dan, *Farm Labourers: Irish Struggle, 1900–1976* (Belfast: Athol Books, 1988)

Brady, A. J. S., *The Briar of Life* (Dublin: Original Writing, 2010)

Brunicardi, Lt Cdr Daire, 'Haulbowline, Spike, and Rocky Islands', Cork Historical Guides Committee, 1969

Brunicardi, Lt Cdr Daire, 'The Ships of the Army, 1922', *An Cosantóir*, vol. 49, no. 3, March 1989, pp. 31–35

Campbell, Colin, Emergency Law in Ireland, 1918-1925 (Oxford: Oxford University Press, 1994)

Clarke, Olga Pyne, *She Came of Decent People* (London: Pelham Books, 1985)

Coleman, Marie, *County Longford and the Irish Revolution, 1910–1923* (Dublin: Irish Academic Press, 2003)

Coogan, Tim Pat, *The Man Who Made Ireland: The Life and Death of Michael Collins* (Niwot, COL: Roberts Rinehart, 1992)

Cottrell, Peter, *The Irish Civil War, 1922–1923* (Oxford: Osprey, 2008)

Creedon, James C., *Cork City Railway Stations, An Illustrated History, 1849–1985* (Cork: Creedon, 1985)

Deasy, Liam, *Brother Against Brother* (Cork: Mercier Press, 1998)

*Dictionary of Irish Biography*, vol. 3 (Cambridge, UK: Cambridge University Press, 2009)

Dolan, Anne and O'Malley, Cormac, *'No Surrender Here!': The Civil War Papers of Ernie O'Malley* (Dublin: Lilliput Press, 2007)

Doyle, Tom, *The Summer Campaign in Kerry* (Cork: Mercier Press, 2010)

*Dublin's Fighting Story, 1916–21* (introduction by Diarmuid Ferriter) (Cork: Mercier Press, 2009)

Duggan, John P., *A History of the Irish Army* (Dublin: Gill & Macmillan, 1991)

Dwyer, T. Ryle, *Tans, Terror, and Troubles: Kerry's Real Fighting Story, 1913–1923* (Cork: Mercier Press, 2001)

Dwyer, T. Ryle, *The Squad and the Intelligence Operations of Michael Collins* (Cork: Mercier Press, 2005)

Foy, Michael, *Michael Collins' Intelligence War: The Struggle Between the British and the IRA, 1919–1921* (London: Sutton, 2006)

Garvin, Tom, *The Birth of Irish Democracy* (Dublin: Gill & Macmillan, 1996)

Hamilton, Nigel, *Monty: The Making of a General, 1887–1942* (New York: McGraw-Hill, 1981)

Harrington, Niall, *Kerry Landing: August 1922* (Dublin: Anvil Books, 1992)

Hart, Peter, *The I.R.A. at War 1916–1923* (London: Oxford University Press, 2003)

Hart, Peter, *The I.R.A. & Its Enemies: Violence and Community in Cork 1916–1923* (Oxford: Oxford University Press, 1998)

Henchion, Richard, *Bishopstown, Wilton and Glasheen: A Picture of Life in the Three Western Suburbs of Cork from Early Days to Modern Times* (Cork: Dahadore, 2001)

Hopkinson, Michael, *Green Against Green: The Irish Civil War* (Dublin: Gill & Macmillan, 1988)

Hurse, A. E., *Monkstown and Passage West* (Cork: Guys, 1929)

Jenkins, Stanley, *The Cork and Muskerry Light Railway* (Cork: Oakwood Press, 1992)

Jenkins, Stanley, *The Cork, Blackrock and Passage Railway* (Cork: Oakwood Press, 1993)

Kissane, Bill, *The Politics of the Irish Civil War* (Oxford: Oxford University Press, 2005)

Linge, John, 'The Royal Navy and the Irish Civil War', *Irish Historical Studies*, vol. 31, no. 121 (May 1998), pp. 60–71

McCarthy, Kieran, *Republican Cobh and the East Cork Volunteers Since 1913* (Dublin: Nonsuch Publishing, 2008)

McIvor, Aidan, *A History of the Irish Naval Service* (Dublin: Irish Academic Press, 1994)

McMahon, Paul, *British Spies and Irish Rebels: British Intelligence and Ireland 1916–1945* (Woodbridge, UK, Boydell Press, 2008)

Neeson, Eoin, *The Civil War in Ireland* (Cork: Mercier Press, 1966)

Neeson, Geraldine, *In My Mind's Eye: The Cork I Knew and Loved* (Dublin: Prestige Books, 2001)

Nyhan, Miriam, *'Are You Still Below?': The Ford Marina Plant, Cork, 1917–1984* (Cork: The Collins Press, 2007)

O'Broin, Leon, *The Revolutionary Underground: The Story of the Irish Republican Brotherhood, 1858–1924* (Dublin: Gill & Macmillan, 1976)

Ó Confhaola, Padhraic, 'The Naval Forces of the Irish State, 1922–1977', PhD dissertation, National University of Ireland, Maynooth, 2009

O'Connor, Emmet, 'Communists, Russia, and the IRA, 1920–1923', vol. 46, no. 1, *The Historical Journal*, 2003

O'Connor, Frank, *An Only Child* (London: Macmillan, 1968)

O'Donoghue, Florence, *No Other Law: The Story of Liam Lynch and the Irish Republican Army, 1916–1923* (Dublin: Anvil Books, 1986)

O'Fáolain, Seán, *Vive Moi!* (London: Sinclair-Stevenson, 1993)

O'Mahony, Colman, *The Maritime Gateway to Cork: A History of the Outports of Passage West and Monkstown, 1754–1942* (Cork: Tower Books, 1986)

Ó Ruairc, Pádraig Óg, *The Battle for Limerick city* (Cork: Mercier Press, 2009)

O'Suilleabhain, Micheal, *Where Mountainy Men Have Sown* (Dublin: Anvil, 1965)

Ó Tuama, Aodh, 'Cork Republican Silver', *Irish Arts Review*, vol. 1, no. 2 (Summer 1984), pp. 52–53

'Padraigh Greene Interview', Ballingeary and Inchigeela Historical Society, *Journal of Ballingeary Cumann Staire*, 2000

Regan, John, *The Irish Counter-Revolution, 1921–1936* (Dublin: Gill & Macmillan, 1999)

Ryan, Meda, *The Day Michael Collins Was Shot* (Dublin: Poolbeg Press, 1989)

Ryan, Meda, *Tom Barry: IRA Freedom Fighter* (Cork: Mercier Press, 2003)

Share, Bernard, *In Time of Civil War: The Conflict on the Irish Railways* (Cork: Collins Press, 2006)

Twohig, Patrick, *Green Tears for Hecuba* (Cork: Tower Books, 1994)

Ungoed-Thomas, Jasper, 'IRA Sectarianism in Skibbereen?', *Skibbereen and District Historical Society Journal*, vol. 6, 2010

White, Gerry and Harvey, Dan, *The Barracks: A History of Victoria/Collins Barracks, Cork* (Cork: Mercier Press, 1997)

Younger, Calton, *Ireland's Civil War* (London: Frederick Muller, 1968)

# INDEX